Mister Bell

A Life Story of Walter D. Bellingrath
Founder of Bellingrath Gardens

by Howard Barney

Published By
THE BELLINGRATH-MORSE FOUNDATION
MOBILE, ALABAMA

Library of Congress Catalog Card No. 78-66291

Printed in the United States of America

for
Mary B.

"If a grain of corn will die and rise again in so much beauty, why may I not die and rise again in infinite beauty and life...."

— from the epitaph
of Walter D. Bellingrath

Walter D. Bellingrath at the age of 80

Foreword

In contemplating the work ahead of him, a biographer of George V expressed concern for his subject's uninteresting and uneventful life. The king, he thought, did little more than hunt and lick rare postage stamps.

I had similar misgivings before beginning this work and injecting myself into the personality of Mister Bell. In the minds of many people, Walter Bellingrath appeared only to make money and enjoy flowers, but the fount of letters and other communications he wrote during a span of 30 years or more belied this conception. His writings reveal not only many interesting facts of his early hardships and simple pleasures but also facets of a complex, fascinating personality whose self-doubts, anxieties and spirituality soften, in retrospect, the crust of his successful business career.

The human interest of Mister Bell's life, in my opinion, overshadows all but his final accomplishment. It is primarily why his story is told in narrative rather than documentary or definitive form, and the reconstruction of it was so absorbing that a sense of personal loss was felt as the final line was written. In death, Mr. Bellingrath seems vastly more vibrant than during my business association with him.

There are omissions, of course, in this story of the co-creator of Bellingrath Gardens. Others might tell it differently and someday may do so, but it is a reasonably complete story of the man, his times and his environment. It is intended to entertain as well as to record the personality of one who kept a promise, made in 1892, to his mother:

". . . by God's help I am going to try to make the world better and brighter by my being here."

There are numerous people to thank, for having helped to make it possible for other generations really to know Mr. Bellingrath and his influence: his mother, Catherine Jean Bellingrath, who thought his letters worth preserving; his niece, Mrs. Jean Bellingrath Lane, for her ten or more years' work on her family genealogy; Mr. Ernest C. Edgar, Jr., for his longtime personal and business association with his Uncle Walter; Mr. George E. Downing, Mr. Bell's close business associate and friend during the last eight years of his life and originator of the idea for this biography; the late Fred W. Holder, for his foresight in taping conversations with early Garden employees and some of Mr. Bellingrath's contemporaries; the late Mr. Harry Sackoff, for his chronicle of the Gardens; and for the delightfully productive hours of reminiscence with people familiar with the man and his life — Mrs. Winona B. Winter, Mrs. Lucy C. Snevely, Miss Ann Crichton; another niece, Mrs. Elmore Bellingrath Bartlett, Mr. Forrest Castleberry, Mr. C. A. L. Johnstone, Jr., Mr. P. D. Beville, Jr., Mrs. Alletta Turner and Mr. Joseph H. Baker.

Finally and emphatically, especial thanks to Mr. Herbert Lyons, for his expert editorial scrutiny and constant encouragement, and to Mrs. Kitty H. Sawyer, who transformed disorderly typing into legibility.

All contributed generously and helpfully to this work of reconstruction. It goes without saying that none of them is in any way responsible for whatever shortcomings the book may have.

And now, Mister Bell!

H. B.
Mobile, Alabama
September 12, 1978

1

THE DRIZZLE of the past 24 hours had become a slashing downpour that arrived horizontally on the raging southeast wind. Streets were deserted, except for the venturesome, the foolhardy, the purposeful.

Among the last ones was a tall, narrow man with shoulders hunched into a wind that further flattened and displaced his thin facial features. His going was slow as he moved into the increasing force and toward his quixotic objective: protection of a fledgling business, frail enough to go under without the help of a hurricane. The street on which he sloshed his way was outlined only by utility poles, awash with the yellow turgid overflow from the nearby river. It also was afloat with creosote paving blocks that drifted with the wind and tide and bumped painfully against the long legs of the solitary figure as he stumbled into shallow holes left by the buoyant blocks.

The year was 1906. The month was hurricane-prone September, and the place was Mobile. Walter Bellingrath wished he lived and worked elsewhere.

He did not like Mobile. "It's an antique metropolis, and its people are antediluvian," he told a friend shortly after his arrival at the Gulf Coast city. And now here he was, a man approaching middle years, with all his savings in an unproven business, faced with the prospect of ruination at the hurricane-powered hands of a God in whom he had unswerving faith.

It was the first time Walter Bellingrath, an inlander, had seen Nature so violent, and it was the worst storm to strike Mobile since 1893. By daylight on September 27, when the worried and anxious Bellingrath struggled to assay his preventive sandbagging of the first floor of his plant, the air was filled

1

with all kinds of flying objects, shutters, signs, roofs, tree limbs, awnings — even chimney bricks. Transmission wires were leveled almost everywhere, and Bellingrath warily avoided contact or entanglement with them.

While he often put his fate in the hands of divine providence, Walter gave Him all assistance possible to safeguard his property against rising waters laden, in addition to paving blocks, with small limbs, lumber, paper and horse manure from the streets and adjacent livery stables.

The hurricane warning system of 1906 was not an "early" one, and communication was only one step removed, he thought, from the tom-tom and smoke signals. Weather flags flown from atop the building occupied by the U. S. Weather Bureau signalled the first alert for most residents of the coastal area, and the city's newcomer learned to read the ominous significance of them, from the initial small craft warning to the two red rectangles with black centers signalling approach of a hurricane.

On the floor just below the flags was the crowded, smoke-filled room of the weather bureau office. Scores of men, including Bellingrath, assembled there in assorted forms of dress, ranging from bowlers and dark "city clothes" to hooded foul weather gear. Their mood was one of nervous jocularity as they conferred with the weatherman and apprehensively watched the barometer drop toward its record low of 28.84. The bureau's prediction that the storm would be centered at Mobile was being confirmed.

The odor of tobacco predominated in the closeness of the office, but with it was mingled the unfamiliar scent of fear emanating from the hot, nervous crowd.

It was this fear and seemingly ceaseless rain that had sent Bellingrath from the confinement of the weather bureau to the vastness of the wet outdoors and the threatening skies above him. On reaching his office a few blocks away, he and a worker unloaded the wagon of its usual merchandise, hitched up the horse and set forth in search of cotton sacks and sand.

As both flood and river waters made their relentless way west, the discouraged business man and his black helper frantically made sandbags and piled them against ground floor openings to the building. It was the first home for his innovative company, and he prayed the Lord would protect it from the pummeling of wind and the harmful effects of high water.

Later, as he waded nearly knee deep to return to his building, Walter Bellingrath was depressed by anxiety, but this same emotion drove him to learn the result of his feeble effort to combat the flood. Furthermore, the office was more of a home to him than the lonely, confining room he occupied in the home of a Mobile family; and, if necessary, he would be safer on the second floor of a strong metal building than at the house where he boarded.

After what seemed a soggy trip to infinity, Bellingrath arrived at his plant to discover water nearly two and a half feet above the threshold. He forced a first floor window and lowered himself into the grayness of the interior. Water was seeping rapidly over and under the sand bags. He raised what he could, but two dynamos were fast disappearing under grease-slick water.

Hands of the wall clock showed nine-thirty, Thursday morning. The storm was at its height, with water being driven in sizeable waves up low lying streets. Suddenly the wind picked up velocity in a dying, roaring effort at destruction. Sound of the wind shut out all other noises, but not the alarming crash of falling bricks and timbers or the frightened cries of his dray animals. Fearing the worst, Bellingrath waded to the stable section to find an old wall and part of the roof had yielded to the hurricane. He led the horse and mule to a safer part of the stable and found they were unhurt.

But not the spirits of W. D. Bellingrath. They were gravely wounded by the storm and damage to his business. He often had been lonesome and homesick since coming to Mobile and being separated from his beloved mother and other family members. Now his depression seemed bottomless, and he reached in his desk for the bottle of solace he sometimes found effective in lifting his mantle of melancholy.

The storm subsided. Waters were receding, as was the Bellingrath anguish. The whiskey not only brought him contentment; it also stirred ripples of nostalgia through his weary brain, ripples that told of other days, happier days.

3

2

LOCKED INESCAPABLY in the memory of Walter Bell-ingrath was Miss Lilly. He remembered her as a quick, bright, impish young woman who "marks that important epoch in my life which is of such vital importance to every individual — the beginning of my accountability, the starting point of my life."

Miss Lilly was his first teacher. She came to Atlanta in 1873, about four years after Walter was born there on August 6, 1869, next to the last of eight children. She was the starting point of his memory, along with the marbles he rolled on the rug of Miss Lilly's school, located in what was then the fairgrounds on Marietta Street. Her pupils consisted primarily of Walter, some of his sisters, brothers, and cousins who lived in a house adjoining the one occupied by young Walter's parents.

The young teacher was as devoted to her charges as Walter was to her and often recalled the joy with which she greeted the bright, fresh faces of the children as they arrived each school day. She taught the rudiments of learning in one small building and lived in another; and Walter, when not thumbing his favorite agate across the floor, sat on a wooden bench at a simple, rectangular table with the other children. And learned to write he did, with a flair, style and eloquence (though it sometimes became verbose) that would characterize the many letters he would write throughout his lifetime to his mother and other family members.

Walter's first known letter, written in block letters on ruled paper, probably under the supervisory eye of Miss Lilly, was to his father, Leonard B. Bellingrath:

Sister Kate and Walter in Atlanta

Dear Papa

I will print you a little letter so you can see how I do at school.

Me want you to get well and come home. Papa bring me some candy when you come.

Your little boy
Walter

It was also at Miss Lilly's that the boy Walter was introduced to one of the loves of his life: singing. It was a pastime that would later brighten otherwise dull evenings in "ragged-edge" rural towns where he would experience twin struggles, earning a livelihood and overcoming boredom and homesickness.

"I can hear her now singing the 'Whipporwill' song and the one about the deer. Wish I was home," he wrote, "so she could sing them again for me . . ."

Miss Lilly, whose last name was Clark, became so endeared to the two Bellingrath families that she moved into Walter's home and taught him and the other children there.

Walter's childish, written plea for his father to come home apparently went unheeded. It was the time of the letter, about 1876 or '77, that his father again began to feel restlessness and discontent with his lot in Atlanta. He was manifesting a form of the same dissatisfaction, even if it was less compelling, that had brought him to Georgia via a long, circuitous route from his European homeland.

3

LEONARD B. BELLINGRATH, the father of Walter, was born April 16, 1832, in Lennep, Germany, a small, medieval village in the Rhine River Valley of northwest Germany. Like his father and a long line of Bellingraths before him, Leonard was destined to become an expert metal worker, particularly in copper cutting and fabrication. Young Leonard did not stick to his copper-smithing. He became entangled in politics (some of his antecedents had held minor political offices) and was caught in the agitation that arose throughout Germany for a freer political order and a closer alliance of the German states.

Shortly before the revolution of 1848, Leonard feared government retaliation for his youthful, rebellious activities and reportedly left Lennep February 28 of that year, under protection of darkness. He is said to have taken only the clothes he wore and carried a passport under an assumed name obtained for him by older friends. Since it was a time of general unrest and uncertainty, many other Germans migrated to the United States in the forties, including Leonard's father, brother Albert and a sister, Henrietta.

After his slow, stormy passage to New York, Leonard stayed briefly with his sister, Henrietta, in New Jersey. He then made his way to Cumberland County, North Carolina, where he joined his father. They worked long hours together in the business of distilling turpentine and making stills for other producers.

Leonard's knowledge of the English language had improved sufficiently in the 1850's for him to go courting. And on September 12, 1855, he and Catherine Jean McMillan said "I do" in a small church at Fayetteville. She was a bride at the

Leonard B. Bellingrath, Walter's German-born father

Catherine McMillan Bellingrath, Walter's mother,
a native of Fayetteville, N.C.

respectable age of 21. Leonard was only 23. It was a happy union that was to result in the birth of Walter and seven other children and develop a full measure of happiness and tragedy.

Even the birth of Walter's mother had forecast the uncertain future of her family and the dramatic events that would affect the lives of all of them. Her birth had been forced by a runaway horse and an overturned buggy. The mother, Catherine Jean Campbell, died as a result of the accident. The baby was reared by its father, William Henry McMillan, and other solicitous relatives.

Only one of Walter's brothers and sisters was born in Cumberland County before Leonard and his family followed the road south to what he hoped would be the greener pasture of Atlanta. He arrived in Georgia well before the War Between the States, fathered two more children there and had another on the way before the outbreak of war. During his fertile period, Leonard attempted to be equally productive in the business of metal working, along with his younger brother, Albert, who also was in Atlanta. His efforts were shortlived.

Having fled one revolution, Leonard soon found himself embroiled in another. His political loyalties were with his adopted Southland, and he joined the 19th Georgia Regiment. Before he could see action, he was put to work in the railroad shops, and later was given the rank of 4th corporal in the Medical Purveyors Guard on May 21, 1864, and was assigned to Company F, 3rd Battalion of the Georgia State Guard. This latter unit was the equivalent of a fire brigade which served only in Fulton County and permitted him and Albert to manufacture saltpeter and alcohol for the Confederate government.

Shortly before Sherman put the torch to Atlanta, Leonard and his family, including a month-old infant son, fled in a boxcar to the area of Cuthbert, Georgia, where another son was born in January, 1866. A few months later, about a year after Lee's surrender, Leonard returned to Atlanta. His immediate venture was the opening of a plumbing business with brother Albert, and W. C. Hunnicut. The family made its home off Marietta Street next door to Albert and his family. This site was then in the country, but the short road on which the two brothers had the only houses was later named Bellingrath Avenue and is now a part of downtown Atlanta.

It was in this home that the last three children of Leonard and Catherine were born: William Albert, 1868; Walter Duncan, 1869; and Catherine Jean, 1871.

4

LEONARD BELLINGRATH was a creative tinkerer. It was not unexpected when he became bored with the mundane business of selling plumbing supplies and equipment. Better judgment urged him to cherish and continue the security of his life in Atlanta, but his emotions listened to a louder and different drummer. After facing the dilemma for several years, Leonard made his decision and grasped an opportunity to return to the turpentine business, with its broader avenues for creativity in design and metal working.

In the late 1870's, Leonard and his wife Catherine packed up their brood of eight. They set forth by train and wagon to the uninviting and unfamiliar hamlet of Castleberry, Alabama, nothing more than a piney-woods crossroads that had once served as a way station operated by an early-generation Castleberry family for horse-drawn coaches traveling the southeast. Leonard Bellingrath became associated with another man in the manufacture and operation of a turpentine still. Castleberry, with its vast pine forests and on the main line of the Louisville and Nashville Railroad, was a productive source of turpentine for the naval stores export business at Mobile, about 90 miles to the south.

Housing of so large a family as the Bellingraths at first was a prickly problem to Leonard and his employer. But it was surmountable. There was a house large enough on the west side of the railroad track, just south of the station, that would not be overly strained by the unforeseen population explosion in the rural Alabama town. Alas, it was occupied on lease to Solomon Castleberry and his family. Negotiations and other manipulations of house trading were begun. Solomon Castleberry would vacate the house if he were provided land and lumber to establish a new home. So agreed, and the large frame house was available to the Bellingraths upon their weary arrival.

Walter Bellingrath once remarked that his teacher, Miss Lilly, occupied "an adjoining chamber in my heart" along with his mother. There certainly was a hurt in that "chamber" upon his being taken at the age of 9 or 10 from the amniotic warmth of his life in Atlanta. His childish eyes first viewed rural Alabama as a forest primeval in contrast to the man-made orderliness of his Georgia surroundings. There was compensation, however, in the new freedom he enjoyed in woods and streams almost within throwing distance of his home.

Walter's brother, Will, was only a year older, and Sister Catherine Jean, nicknamed Katie, was only two years younger. The trio had many happy times, but division of the sexes occurred when Walter and Will momentarily found relief from summer's heat by skinny dipping in the nearby creek. It was a delight occasionally interrupted by the frightening sight of water moccasins dropping into the water from overhanging foliage, incidents that always sent Walter and friends scurrying to land.

The creek was a summertime mecca for older boys, as well as the young Bellingraths. It was then that Walter found swimming to be a new pinnacle of pleasure. He dived off their shoulders, and they threw him playfully from the bank, or improvised diving platforms, from which the boy would do his "preacher seats". And it was from the older lads that Walter learned the difference between swimmers and "bank walkers." The latter, he jokingly recounted many years later, were the boys who showed unabashed pride in their masculinity.

It was in these same waters that Walter, as a young teenager, began a hobby he would enjoy throughout life. A stick fishing pole was his frequent companion. Worms and crickets were plentiful, as were the bream and gargle eye to help Mother Catherine fill the seemingly bottomless stomachs of her children.

Freedom enjoyed by the children in Castleberry offered many pleasures, but it was not without some pain. One Sunday, while en route home from church, Walter and Will stopped to play at a sawmill, despite frequent admonitions from their mother against the dangerous area. While frolicking, Walter had a piece of sharp, heavy metal fall on his hand. The tip of his middle finger was severed. The boys located a can, filled it with turpentine and, using a popular first-aid remedy of the day, immersed the injured finger in the fluid to stop bleeding. The accident resulted in a shorter finger with a stunted nail.

In 1883, Walter and Katie attended the "Castleberry Male & Female School." They both were in the top form, the grammar school; and Will presumably had moved on to high school. A report card, dated November 20, gave the names of all pupils at the school and their relative rank in scholarship, attendance and deportment.

There were only nine other children in the grammar school with the two Bellingrath youngsters. Forecasting his aptitudes, Walter was number three in his class in scholarship. He had a 9.4 grade out of a possible 10. Deportment? His characteristic mischievousness and fondness for devilment already were showing. Only Sister Katie had a lower level of deportment. A total of 22 children attended the primary and intermediate departments of the school, which must have seemed congested to them in contrast to the exclusiveness of Miss Lilly's.

5

THE EARLY LIFE of Walter Bellingrath in the backwoods of Castleberry was not all fun and games. In his sixteenth year, he began to feel the adolescent desire for more independence and freedom from family restraints, as well as a wish to have his own money. Since the Louisville and Nashville, with its mighty engines moving freight to faraway places, appeared to present the biggest opportunity for a youngster of 16, Walter decided on a career of railroading.

He prevailed upon the local station agent at Castleberry to teach him telegraphy. Having a musical ear and a sense of rhythm, he became proficient in operating the brass telegrapher's key in a relatively short time. Walter's first job, as he began his Horatio Alger climb, was as night telegraph operator at Brewton, a few miles down the L & N from his home.

For the next few years, Walter moved about the state in various railroad jobs. It was Anniston in 1889, as night operator and ticket agent for the old Georgia Pacific Railroad, and later, another railroad, at an unidentified Alabama town, as day operator and revising clerk.

Like Walter at the time, the head of the Bellingrath household also felt the need to move beyond the unproductive limits of Castleberry. Fire had destroyed his turpentine still, and the operation was brought to a halt. Older brother Albert Bellingrath, still in business in Atlanta, sent a large shipment of clothes and provisions to keep the family going until Leonard could recover from his financial losses. Leonard took to the road as a traveling salesman of supplies and equipment for the turpentine industry. He also attempted to develop another turpentine still in the New Orleans area and wrote Walter, January 29th, 1892:

> . . . I have the house nearly half up, weatherboarded and hope to finish it next week entire. I will get all my dry lumber for stills and tub tomorrow, and will commence working on them Monday.
>
> The copper for the still is here, the copper pipes are nearly finished, the boiler will be finished next week, and we have the bill of lading for the . . . engine.
>
> Our four driven wells are finished, they are 71 foot deep and will furnish 3000 gallons of water an hour, but the water is salt; so we will have to dig a well six feet square and fifteen feet deep to get fresh water for the boiler . . .
>
> I have hired a coppersmith at 4.00 per day and he is to furnish all his own tools . . .
>
> Mama has seen considerable of the city this week, has also been to the Lake, but she will explain herself in her own happy way. I have nothing of interest to write as I leave in the morning and don't get back before night . . .
>
> Your affectionate father,
>
> L.B.

Walter received this letter in Anniston. It was one of the last he would get from the father who had worked so arduously, if capriciously, for the welfare of his large family. In his final illness, an ailment reportedly brought on by prolonged inhalation of turpentine fumes, Leonard mentally returned to his Lennep homeland. He reverted to his native language before he died on October 7, 1892.

Leonard's death coincided with his youngest son's proud return to Castleberry as agent for the L & N. Walter rented a room in their old Castleberry home along the tracks, and ghosts of his happy boyhood there, coupled with grief, summarily nullified the pride felt for his new job. Walter wrote his mother:

> I have had the blues a little worse than expected . . . you know coming back here and living in the same old house, where we lived so long and happy, makes it worse on me than if I had gone into a strange community. Everyone seems awful glad to see me, and in fact each one has told me on the sly that they had not had as accommodating an agent as I was since I left here.

This sotter bouys a fellow up, but I will not allow myself to get drunk on flattery . . .

I get along ok in the daytime but at night I get lonesome, and then my thoughts fly homeward . . . I wish it were possible for us to see and talk to papa once more, and tell him the many nice things that were said about him and how he has been missed from our midst. . . Oh, mama, it is then I realize how good he was and how he was appreciated while here, even though little demonstration was made on the part of those who respected and loved him. What a pity it is we all don't try and tell each other how we love one another while we can. . .

Walter's mother and Katie had moved to Anniston following Mr. Bellingrath's death to be with some of the other children who lived there.

The railroad station at Castleberry, which was to be home for Walter for two years or more, was a prototype of the rectangular buildings which punctuated the tracks of southern railroads: a frame building with peaked roof, narrow platforms on each side and a larger one for freight at an end. The interior was divided into two small offices and larger space for passengers and freight needing protection from the weather. The name CASTLEBERRY shouted, with an intensity greater than the importance of the stop, from a large wooden name plate at each end of the station.

But in Walter's outlook, there was no belittling the agent's job. The work and $75 a month earnings promptly lifted Walter from his doldrums. The physical exercise of trucking cotton and other heavy freight improved the muscle tissue, as well as mental attitude, of the 23-year-old. His muscle "swelled to about twice its size," and so did his religious convictions.

The gift of a Bible from his adored Kate prompted Walter to comment that since his father's death, he had more religious faith than ever before. He saw in that sad event the significance of religion. "I don't think it possible for anyone to go through with what he did without the grace of God." He found, too, a comparison in the life of Christ and his father and thought of them as "two journeying along together, each sharing his part of the burden without a single complaint and with a smile always on their meek faces."

17

Walter's moods were mercurial, however, and his sense of humor often rose to the surface when his thoughts were deep, his spirits low. No sooner did he speak of his father's death and profess his strong religious beliefs than he told Kate:

"You will have to wait until I strike the Louisiana State lottery before I can reciprocate. Nice talk, isn't it, for a fellow who's just received a Bible."

A short time later, he salved or cured a heartache by inquiring about the aging of Miss Lilly and another friend:

"I hope they are not in the same pew with the old man who was courting a young widow. He remarked: 'Betsy, I can jump the fence as easy as I ever could.' But asks she, 'Can you jump it as often?'"

The young railroad agent was basically serious-minded and a young man of strong purpose. He often was at his bare-walled station until late at night, when it was so quiet he could "almost hear myself think." If not shifting freight, working on his bills of lading and other records, all written by hand with thin yellow tissues for copies, he dreamed of ways to supplement his income. He marked cotton for an extra $10 a month and garnered a small monthly fee from a young man for teaching him the clerical duties of a railroad agent's job.

The money-making idea which gave him most pleasure — gastronomically speaking — was the buckets of oysters he had shipped to him from Mobile. "After eating all I could, I sold one and cleared $1.80." He then asked his brother Will to send him the name of a company that produced paper oyster cartons and the price per dozen. Walter did not live on oysters alone:

"My hash is only costing me $12.50, and I have old 'No. 9' washing for me," he said in discussing his cost of living in the fall of '92. Yet oysters, whether his own or others, patently were his favorite food.

"I went to Brewton last night and ate about a barrel of oysters. Today I have the tub ache, and as you have such a big one," he told a portly friend, "I suppose you know what that is." A limited amount of "hash" and fat-free oysters obviously agreed with Walter: More than six feet tall, he weighed less than 130 pounds at the time and was elated that so many people thought his long thin face, with prominent nose and ears to match, closely resembled that of his deceased father.

Walter's Christmas in Castleberry without his family was one of dejection and meditation. Old friends in the community attempted to cheer him. But sadness over his first Christmas without papa and the length and strength of the Silver Cord were stronger than the extended hands of his neighbors.

"It makes tears come in my eyes to think that he can never wish us another Merry Christmas and Happy New Year. Christmas eve when I lay down I wondered what you all were doing at home and what you were going to fix for papa. Christmas morning when I got up, it was not with the light heart I had carried on that morning for 22 years but a sad heart because I knew you all were not happy and could not be with papa not with you."

His letter to his mother continued: "And when I came out to find everybody happy and rejoicing it only made me the sadder." He reported some consolation, nevertheless, in gifts of sheet music, cake and nuts from his family, as well as his father's watch sent to him via an older sister from his mother.

"The train has blew for the station so will come to an abrupt close . . ." The letter was signed, "your baby boy, Walter".

The train whistle was blowing. But not many more whistles would Walter answer there. Each brought him nearer to the time when Castleberry was just a memory.

6

WALTER BELLINGRATH'S next move was to the Georgia Southern & Florida Railroad. While he anticipated an advancement in his career, his first assignment was more like the end of the line. He was fast running out of track, he thought, as he sweltered through the long months of the summer of '94 in a boxcar station at the hamlet of Richwood, Georgia, about 30 miles east of Plains, a long way from anywhere.

The stultifying routine of his life in this remote area was responsible for Walter's introduction to alcohol. It served infrequently as an escape hatch for the bored railroad agent and was particularly pleasurable when drunk with one of two of his rural cronies to the accompaniment of the harmonica Walter always had close at hand. As he told a friend, "I like the way it tastes. I like the way it smells. And I like the way it makes me feel."

The young man had more than enough time for self-examination while on his first job with the Georgia Southern. His introspection began to be evident in future communications and relationships with his family and friends he met on down the line.

Down the line actually was up for Walter Bellingrath, as the railroad elevated him to station agent at Jasper, Florida. It was a town that seemed a teeming city to Walter in contrast to Richwood and its boxcar ambiance.

"I am very much better pleased here than I have been in sometime," he wrote, and enthusiastically told of his planned visit to Suwanee Springs and of the opportunity to see the river "we have so often sung about."

"When I look at it will think of you old mountain yaps [in Anniston, Alabama] and pity you for having no such sights."

Walter arrived at Jasper shortly before August 6, 1894, when "old Father Time edged me off the quarter century mark of my allotted time on this terrestial globe." In many ways, his 25th birthday signalled the advent of the adult life and times of Walter Bellingrath. His seasoning at Richwood apparently brought major changes in the young man, made him more eager to extend his reach and to become more involved in human relationships that would enhance his own happiness.

During this period, Walter initially displayed few if any signs of overconfidence or vanity. He often weighed himself "in the balances, and I am sorry to say from my standpoint I am generally found wanting. I don't know if my scales register the same in everyone elses eyes as mine or not. If they do, I am making poor headway. I sometimes feel that I have accomplished a right smart and again I don't know. . . ."

Walter was settling down, finding himself. He vowed to make a new start in Jasper. Encouragement from a railroad superior helped him to reach a major decision:

"I have about decided to make RR my business, and from this time on I am going to try and let each succeeding year find me further up . . . the ladder than the one I left behind me."

Not only his ambition, but Walter's zest for living also was on the upswing. He joined a church choir and regularly attended Sunday School or Bible classes, started soliciting freight for the railroad, and got to know many of the thousand or more residents of the Jasper area. Most of these people he found to be unattractive "crackers," but many were to his liking. He became enmeshed in the small-town social life of the town lying about midway between Tallahassee and Jacksonville, close to the Georgia border. Recreation was simple but satisfying and in keeping with customs of the times and folkways of the area. Walter particularly enjoyed choir singing and rehearsals, with attendant frolicking with two girls who sang with him, Bethulia and "Miss Willie".

Sugar cane replaced Mobile Bay oysters as young Bellingrath's favorite food; he ate it nearly every day in season and found it particularly enjoyable while swinging on the front porch of Bethulia's large white house. At other times, Bethulia used homemade ice cream, mounds of it, as a way to Walter's heart.

Miss Bethulia Rice was Walter's first love. About 18 or 19 years old, she was small, slender, of pale complexion with dark hair and eyes that matched her suitor's slate blue. She was a modest young lady, but Walter admired her mental quickness. "Sharp as a brier and better versed than myself." Bethulia also was slightly aloof, and, in Walter's eyes, of pedestal quality. She played the piano well, prompting the starry-eyed young man to write home for some of his favorite music. He and a couple of his male friends often enlivened things by serenading Bethulia and other young ladies of the town. One of his favorite serenade songs was "Only Flirting," which he taught to the other singers after getting the words from his sister, Kate.

Bethulia's stepfather owned the town's leading drug store, was a Yankee, Republican and had been married several times. "But one thing is certain," Walter said, "it will take worse than his politics, religion or profession to keep me away from his house."

The parent was successful, however, in enforcing on Walter a distasteful curfew. The hour of 10 o'clock arrived too quickly for him. It was extremely difficult for him to say good night, but except on special occasions he always managed to leave at the specified hour.

Early hours, being in love and a diet of sugar cane and ice cream manifestly agreed with Walter. In two weeks of courting Bethulia, his weight was up from 130 pounds to 135, much to the delight of a young man eager to put more pounds on his gangling frame.

Good health, as well as love and Miss Bethulia, combined forces as a catalyst for the furtherance of Walter's program of self-education. His apparent envy of her superior knowledge and her reputation as the school poet inspired Walter to return to some of the classics, principally Dickens, and also to read more poetry. One of the books lent him by his young sweetheart was the "First Violin", a story that put the amateur critic in mind of Dickens' writings. Walter considered Jessie Fathergill's characters to be of a higher class than the Dickens ones. At about the same time, Walter was engrossed in "A Tale of Two Cities," a story which he considered to be superior to the "Old Curiosity Shop," preferring the "more genial characters" of the former and its more entertaining text.

"But neither Dickens nor Fathergill is me lady," said Walter in tribute, no doubt, to the meter and style of Bethulia's high school poetry.

A voracious reader at this time, Walter looked forward to receiving each week the *Sunday School Times*. Nearly always the short lectures and lesson explanations in that periodical helped him prepare his own Sunday School lessons. He subscribed to the publication for 10 weeks at a cost of a penny a week.

Neither that item on his expense ledger nor his love for Bethulia dimmed his feeling of responsibility for his own family. One older brother was having difficulty finding a job at the time, and the youngest son felt responsible for the financial welfare of his mother and younger sister in Anniston. He and brother Will provided the security needed by the Anniston family. In August of 1894, Walter told Will that on payday he had a $15 surplus but did not wish to remit all he had, so was sending $10 home with the tentative assurance he could contribute at least $30 on his next payday. In October his monthly contribution reached a peak of $45.

The lean times and ceaseless hard work young Bellingrath experienced with the railroads taught him a lesson he would never forget and often put into practice during his lifetime: the value of a dollar should never be regarded lightly. An early demonstration of this monetary philosophy was a head-on collision with the Express Company. It wanted him to pay for a year's bonding premium. Walter concluded he was liable for only one month, since he had broken his connection with the company after the first month.

"I believe I have the company in a hole, and if they don't

steal it out of my commissions, don't think they will ever get the year's premium", he said.

"If they do, I will be out another $5."

7

MANHOOD, with its customary blend of pleasures and burdensome responsibilities, was rapidly overtaking young Walt. He loved Thulia, devotedly so, but the weight of family problems began to enshroud him and dampen the glow of his really first romance. For many months, he became preoccupied with money, his lack of it, and his interest in death and the hereafter was gloomily rekindled by the impending demise of his brother Edwin, the first-born of Leonard and Catherine Bellingrath.

Times — even Christmas time — became relatively hard for Walter Bellingrath. His Christmas gift to his mother and Kate was not sent until January because, as he apologized:

"I didn't have the *stuff* Christmas."

The belated stuff was a money order for $22.50. Of this, $17.50 was specified for their rent, and $2.50 was Christmas for his mother and an equal amount for his sister.

A mortgage on a parcel of property owned by Mrs. Bellingrath was due in early '95, much sooner than Walt had anticipated. The physician who had attended Leonard Bellingrath during his long illness was pressing the family for a settlement of the account. Uncle Albert also should be paid for funds advanced to his brother's family during their lean years. Walter felt the oppression of these and other creditors upon his narrow shoulders. His efforts to borrow $75 from a Castleberry friend on a six-months note finally were successful. The money was needed as his share of the mortgage interest.

Walter's concern over his inability to help finance his mother's debts was intensified and magnified by illness. He was greatly behind in his work, with this adding to his anxiety over futile efforts to pacify a nagging conscience by fulfilling filial responsibility to his mother. Yet out of the chaotic uncertainty and indecision came a solution. The mother would deed her remaining Atlanta property to Thede, Will and Walter, if they would erase the three-year-old indebtedness.

"I am perfectly willing," Walter wrote ". . . provided it is agreeable to Thede and Will. One thing certain, if Dr. Gaston's account is not settled soon, he is going to put us to a great deal of trouble . . . . We will set in at once to try to get rid of these accounts. I think the doctor's bill unreasonable but suppose it's useless to say anything about it now. It will push me to pay him anything and meet my share of the interest note but guess I will be able to do so by making an extra effort."

Walter considered the property his mother proposed to give her sons to be worth less than the obligation they would assume. He agreed, however, there was nothing else to be done since Mrs. Bellingrath was insolvent.

That was Walter Bellingrath's introduction to the intricacies and vicissitudes of banking and finance. However, it was a cloud-lining that certainly went unrecognized by the harried young man.

For Walter during his Florida residency, there naturally were depressed days, as well as harried and elated ones. He was vocal about such moments and related his emotions to the death of his father in 1892 and the illness of Edwin.

> As I think of the many changes that have come to the family since then I feel anything but happy. I sometimes think it well he went when he did, and then I think had he lived, many things would not have happened that have . . . he is in heaven where he is far happier and better off than he could possibly be here.
>
> With this in mind, I often make new resolution and set off with new purposes to live as he did that when I come to die I may know I am going to a better world, where I'll meet him and all my loved ones.

Walter was about 12 years younger than his brother Edwin and was not as close to him as to the younger brothers. Also, Edwin had a prolonged illness. Consequently, Walter was not as emotionally involved in his death as he was in his father's.

He wrote of "poor old Ed" and what a happy release death must be for him.

"Now that he is at rest, I feel more at ease about him than I have since he was afflicted, as I now know he is beyond all earthly suffering and in Heaven."

While he may have viewed Ed's death in an impersonal way, Walter found the sad event cause for him again to express almost rapturous feelings for his overall relationship to his family. Thede, in writing Walter "a beautiful letter" about Ed, also described how brother Will had stood by the ill man in such a noble, helpful manner.

"It made my blood tingle," Walter responded, "as I read such earnest expressions from one brother to another. He spoke of Ed in the tenderest terms, and it made my heart swell and my eyes fill to read the words which I knew had come from the heart of one so true and noble. And . . . Bill in his letters spoke so sweet and comforting . . . To have such brothers is an honor, and may the bonds of love which have withstood the trials of this life so far remain unbroken till we are gathered home over yonder."

8

WALTER'S YEARS in Jasper were profitable and productive ones. Not monetarily, of course, but his social experiences and job training contributed generously to his emerging maturity. The results of his continuing self-education, largely prompted by the aloof superiority of Bethulia Rice, were readily recognized in his correspondence. His grammar improved, his vocabulary burst into bloom, and his correspondence became so eloquent and discursive that inspiration for his nocturnal writings may have come from other than Miss Bethulia.

The Georgia Southern also gave its agent an opportunity to broaden his horizon, a vacation with railroad passes to Chicago. "I think I can go and spend a couple of days for $5," he said in making plans for the journey.

Jasper also presented Walter with his first sales and marketing experience and exposed him to the workings of distributorships and other middle men. His first comprehensive, indoctrinating taste of the trials and frustrations of being boss also was roughly spooned to him while he was with the Georgia Southern.

"My assistant is a cheap man and like most cheap things cannot be depended upon. He pretended he was sick last week, and the two days I was most eager to have him were the very ones he was absent. He has been of little service to me for the past month, and yesterday I gave him a straight talk. This a.m. he resigned which pleased me, as I did not like to discharge him. I preferred he do just as he did.

"You know, there are plenty more to be had."

Years later, Walter Bellingrath paraphrased this assertion with the familiar admonition, "Fish or cut bait."

It was mid-1897 when Walter decided he would rather fish in other waters. Life was pleasant, he had to admit, in Jasper with Bethulia. His more pressing financial problems, including payment of his share of Ed's burial expenses, were more or less behind him. But Walter repudiated his earlier decision: railroading would not be his career. He'd had enough and looked forward to ending his three years in the sleepy Florida town, along with the day-to-day wrestling of heavy freight, looking up routes for unpleasant "crackers" and soliciting cargo. Walter's ambition, his romantic ardor and desire for matrimony, accelerated the falling sands of his time in Jasper. Before submitting his resignation, he looked about for other opportunities, fixing his eyes stonily on his pocketbook. More income was needed to put "Bethulia's shoes under my bed."

Wishing to live closer to members of his family, the 28-year-old Bellingrath made plans to move to Montgomery, Alabama, to go in business for himself, as a broker of grain and other provisions.

Goodbyes to Thulia were both prolonged and emotional, with the Rices' swing and davenport occupied with greater frequency and often past the paternal 10 o'clock curfew. Dramatic vows were exchanged, with Belshazzar (as she initially called him) solemnly and mistily pledging to keep her always in an exclusive chamber of his heart and to keep the postal service busy with messages of adoration.

Finally, Walter wrenched himself from Bethulia's charms and the routine and comfort of Jasper for a new life in Montgomery.

9

THE CHANGE that developed in Walter Bellingrath's personality during his years in Montgomery was nearly as noticeable and clear-cut as his break with railroading and the serenity of life at Jasper. He embraced the philosophy that he could not afford to fail and became successful as a merchandise broker.

"I am now into this thing, and I have got to succeed. You don't know what you can do until you get a bull by the horns and can't turn loose."

His thoughts of Bethulia and his innate acquisitiveness drove him forward. And from his accomplishments came the shining self-confidence and vanity often found on the personality escutcheons of self-made men.

His first employee, a man of 42, always addressed the under-30 Walter as "Boss."

"You can tell from his manner and attitude toward me that he has only respect for me, and in calling me 'Boss' he means no ridicule. I am not . . . vanity proof and when my employee honors me . . . I feel a breeze waft through the heart strings of my vanity and immediately thereafter a tingling sensation goes all over me, and it is only with an effort I keep a profuse blush from mounting my *modest* and swarthy cheek."

The young businessman reflected, with pride and some amusement, on his "unmitigated nerve" in undertaking the brokerage venture. Walter found it almost unbelievable, even unthinkable, that he paid a hired man $100 a month when he had never received a salary of that amount during his years with the railroads.

Walter and an unidentified friend visit a Montgomery photographic studio shortly after he entered the brokerage business in that city in the late 1890's.

During one of the earlier months, the fledgling brokerage business grossed $165 during a 15-day period. Its owner expected earnings of that amount during the last half of the month, permitting him also to draw $100. Walter regretted that administrative demands of the office kept him off the street and prevented him from supplementing the sales work of his assistant.

"My hired man is a much better salesman than myself . . . but I can walk all over him when it comes to taking care of my correspondence. As the pen is said to be mightier than the sword, you will at once realize the necessity of having a massive brain and eagle eye at the head of this branch of the business," he once said with tongue not too deep in cheek.

Nearly all of Walter's time was devoted to his new business. As months passed his demonstrative devotion to the girl he left behind began to fade. Preoccupation with commerce and his business correspondence was so consuming that his sworn vow to write regularly to Bethulia was overlooked. Both time and distance took their toll. Her silence — not even a Dear John Letter — left Walter distraught. A box of Huyler's candy sent to her, with a pleading note seeking forgiveness, was ignored, leaving the hopeful sender the annoying uncertainty as to whether she had actually received it.

Bellingrath's uncertainty over Bethulia's feelings for him was heightened by a visit to Montgomery of an old friend from Jasper. Walter later told of memories rekindled by the visit:

> My love affair, like all others when looked at from a personal standpoint, is not an ordinary case. Hence, when my pilgrim friend brought before me the scenes of my first love, I, like most other culprits, fell into line and eagerly drank in all the news he brought . . . sufficient to fan the embers of this desolate heart of mine into a congenial glow. I neglected my ecclesiastical duties for the first time in a long while and devoted myself and attention to him and a review of what had happened in the old town since I had seen it last.
>
> His visit was delightfully pleasant, with just enough romance reference to my past life, which he knows well, to fasten upon me a solemn fascination for those good old days that are now gone forever.
>
> For one to be associated with "Tudy" was an intellectual treat. As I look back I see where she was the direct cause of

Walter with a customer in his Montgomery office

me having an ambrosial time on a number of occasions and now realize the time I spent in that little ragged edge town with her the center of attraction for me will make up a large proportion of the halcyon days of my life.

Just as the shades of evening announced the close of another day, my friend boarded the car for his home. I bid him adieu and watched the train make its start for the Land of Flowers carrying my friend and my heart with it. When it had disappeared, I found myself possessed with a longing which nothing would satisfy . . . and my anxiety darkened into despair.

Walter's sense of humor saved his heart from shattering. He admitted he tore his breeches by not writing at least once a month and said she "drew the line."

"I can't hollow down her rain barrel, nor slide down her cellar door no more . . . ."

After this final clutch at the happy past, and believing he never would hear from her again, Walter immersed himself in work rather than regret and continued his efforts to increase his earnings beyond the $100 a month he proudly wrote home about.

10

AT ABOUT THE TIME Walter Bellingrath was making a new start in Montgomery, an innovative idea was sinking its roots into the mind of a fellow southerner. It was to have a decisive effect on the destiny of Walter and other members of his immediate family.

Benjamin Franklin Thomas, a resident of Chattanooga, where he was both a lawyer and business man, was serving his stint in the commissary department of the U. S. Army in Cuba during the Spanish-American War. He observed Cubans readily buying bottles of a carbonated drink with a pineapple base. Thomas had formed a liking at home for a product called Coca-Cola, then available only at a typically American institution known as the soda fountain. There were times, of course, when a fountain was not near by, and Thomas would have enjoyed a drink of the beverage introduced in Atlanta 14 years before in 1886 by a prominent pharmacist, John S. Pemberton.

Thomas carried the bottling idea in his mind until the end of hostilities and his return to Chattanooga. The more he thought of the idea, the more feasible it became. He passed these thoughts on to a friend, Joseph Brown Whitehead. The latter also was a lawyer with something of a promoter's mind, and he enthusiastically endorsed Thomas' idea of bottling Coca-Cola.

Since the project depended upon obtaining permission of The Coca-Cola Company, the pair of nineteenth century promoters traveled to Atlanta. They obtained an interview with Asa G. Candler, who had acquired ownership of Coca-Cola over a three-year period for a cash outlay of $2,300, plus some exchange of proprietary products produced by his pharmacy.

Candler was married to the idea of Coca-Cola's future being

35

at the soda fountain, not in bottles. He showed no more enthusiasm for the proposal of his visitors than he did a few years previously when a Vicksburg confectioner privately bottled Coca-Cola, along with other flavors, in the back room of his store. Joseph A. Biedenharn, who shipped his bottled drink from Vicksburg, to country customers, acted with Candler's knowledge but without his encouragement. In fact, Biedenharn sent his first case of two dozen bottles to the president of Coca-Cola, who acknowledged the gift by commenting "that it was fine." Candler did not elaborate. He failed also to return the case of bottles.

Thomas and Whitehead received the same indifferent response as the confectioner until they repeatedly assured Coca-Cola's "sole proprietor" that they would assume full responsibility for the new undertaking. Candler finally agreed to a contract, a document of only 600 words, dated July 21, 1899, granting the two men the right to bottle Coca-Cola and distribute it in all parts of the United States excepting six New England states, Texas and Mississippi. The exclusion was for various legal reasons.

Thomas and Whitehead returned to Chattanooga justifiably elated but without realizing the potential results of their contract: the new industry it would originate and its effect on the destinies of so many people, including Walter D. Bellingrath.

Back in Montgomery, fate was looking favorably on the young merchandise broker. His thinking may not have been on the same plateau with the Chattanooga innovators, but his business was progressing satisfactorily. And much of the uncertainty and unrest attending so large a family as his had quieted. His Sister Kate was recently married; his older sister, Mary Elizabeth, was comfortably settled with a good husband and children; his three brothers all had jobs; his mother was happy in Anniston and Miss Lilly was living with her. When Walter wrote home, it often was with tender thoughts of Miss Lilly as well as of his mother.

One of his only irritations, and one which inspired a short burst of temper, was the failure of some relatives to acknowledge properly the money Walter regularly sent to them for his maternal Grandpa's expenses.

"For instance, I have never heard a word from them this

year. I of course do not expect Grandpa to write. He is too old and has to depend on others. Yet it does seem that some of them could afford to take time to acknowledge receipt of my remittances."

Walter was irked but continued to send money. He was quick of temper but equally quick to forget, particularly when the cause for anger came from relatives or friends.

The orderly channel of Walter's career and life in Montgomery was headed, however, for an uncharted shoal, which would change the course of his future. His brother Will, only a year older than Walter, left the Woodstock Iron Company, with headquarters in Anniston, when the company decided to close down indefinitely.

This was the spring of 1903. The two brothers always had desired a joint business venture (one earlier plan had aborted), and this appeared to be the propitious time to undertake it. Walt's brokerage business would not support them both, so Will began to look beyond grain and provisions. He was nearly as observant as the U. S. Army officer in Cuba and had noticed the popularity, steadily on the rise, of bottled soft drinks among Woodstock mine workers and tenders of the blast furnaces. Will had no difficulty in selling his brother on the idea of buying the then available Montgomery franchise for Coca-Cola. But there was difficulty in raising the necessary funds to buy the company from C. V. Rainey. After repeated disappointments and setbacks, the brothers did borrow enough to supplement their savings and acquire the property in June, 1903. Since it required about $5,000 at the turn of the century to equip an average-size bottling plant, it is believed the brothers invested about $5,000 each in the already established plant.

Showing the business acumen and foresight that was to be responsible for the business success of the brothers, they bought also the franchise of the Mobile Coca-Cola Bottling Company from Crawford Johnson of Birmingham. The Mobile franchise was acquired by the two Bellingraths in September, 1903.

11

BY THE TIME Walter Bellingrath invested his future in Mobile, the city was being dethroned by Birmingham as Alabama's largest and most influential. Cotton had ended its monarchial reign, and less and less of it moved down the Tombigbee, Alabama and Mobile Rivers to the state's only seaport. Not only had river traffic dwindled, but an enlarged southern railroad system diverted cotton and other raw materials to eastern ports or to New Orleans.

Mobile's transient population, including theatrical and musical groups, also declined in the late nineteenth and early twentieth centuries. Years before, Mobile's theaters, restaurants and other attractions were mecca for upriver planters and their families. The lights of Mobile's theaters then shone on some of the nation's most famous actors and musicians. But by 1903, the port city was no longer a hub of cultural and social activity for the southeast.

Mobile had become a sleepy southern city of fewer than 40,000 people and was isolated from most of the socio-economic forces strengthening the industrial muscles of the burgeoning nation. But to the 34-year-old Bellingrath, late of Castleberry, Richwood, Jasper and Montgomery, Mobile was truly the metropolis he described it shortly after his arrival there. The city had new-fangled electric street cars. It already had said farewell in 1902 to the last of the mule-drawn trolleys (the Toulminville-Lafayette Street run), and the first modern street paving had been laid to replace some of the creosote block, brick and cobblestone streets.

Mobile may have been somnolent, but it offered a fertile, compatible environment for the start of Walter's bottling com-

Walter Bellingrath's first bottling plant, immediately after the disastrous 1906 hurricane

pany. The city's culture was affected by its omnipresent waterfront. An expression of this culture was the inability of anyone to travel more than a block or two within the city's mile-square limits without being able to buy a drink of whiskey. There may have been only one theater in Mobile, but there were more than 100 saloons, a total slightly less than half the number of grocery stores. The latter were supplemented by numerous delicatessens, cook shops and stalls, all potential outlets for products of the Mobile Coca-Cola Company, W. D. Bellingrath, president. There was only one other legitimate bottling company doing business in the city when he and Will bought the Mobile operation for $10,000.

In addition to bottling the revolutionary new drink, Coca-Cola, with its secret formula the subject of early suspicion, the Bellingrath company made ginger ale, soda waters, seltzer, mineral waters and sold chewing gum, julep straws and "Pratt's famous crystal brand liquid gas."

Despite the potential of the Mobile market, it was elusive, and the struggles of Walter Bellingrath during his first year in the port city are almost legendary. He worked extremely long hours in and out of his first little plant on Water Street near St. Louis Street, which he occupied until about the end of 1906. He sometimes pondered the source of his next meal and was so "perplexed" by his reception in Mobile that he forgot his mother's 69th birthday, for the first time since he had learned to count. He wrote in apology:

"What a fellow without a mother does when the world gets him down and rolls on top of him I can't imagine. To get a couple of letters like those you wrote me, when one is lonesome and homesick, is worth more than money — because you give to a hungry heart a mother's love and sympathy, something filthy lucre can't buy. . . ."

Walter began business with one mule, a wagon, a black helper and a primitive hand and foot-powered bottling machine initially capable of producing only a few cases per hour. Walt would bottle one day, wearing heavy gloves, leather apron and a face mask to protect himself against exploding glass. A low pressure bottling system had not been developed. The next day, he and his helper would drive the wagon about the city making deliveries, with Walt giving his sales pitch to saloon

A delivery wagon used by Walter Bellingrath in the early 1900's

keepers, restaurant operators and nearly every other potential dealer who would pause to listen. After selling his soft drinks, Walter then would retrieve most of the bottles, wash them by hand and refill them for the next day's delivery. Not until the business became more successful did he have enough money for surplus bottles.

Walter Bellingrath actually began business with a bottle shortage, having received less than his due from the previous owner. Enclosed metal shipping cases for three dozen bottles were used in those days. To check the cases for bottles, the new buyer looked in slots at each end, saw glass and assumed the cases were full. On later removing tops of the containers, he found many of the bottles missing, a production handicap he found difficult to overcome.

The large metal cases were used by Walter to ship Coca-Cola and other soft drinks by rail and river boat to upcountry saw mills and plantations. This market proved to be an unexpected source of revenue for the struggling bottler, and he devoted much of his evening hours to correspondence to develop this facet of the business. When the wagon was in use by his helper, Walter sometimes was seen putting his railroad experience to work. The waterfront was only two blocks away, and he found delivering a couple of shipping cases of soft drinks on a hand truck or dolly easier than moving a bale of cotton at Castleberry. Usually waiting alongside the Mobile River piers to receive Bellingrath's shipments were the river packets *Mary, Nettie Quill* or *James T. Staples,* which still served as the principal means of transportation to hundreds of upstate landings.

Walter found the considerable early sales resistance to Coca-Cola perplexing and frustrating. He believed wholeheartedly in his product. It infuriated him whenever someone questioned the quality of the drink or ignorantly contended that it contained drugs. In fact, some Mobilians were as suspicious of Coca-Cola as they were of another product being advertised at the time:

"Smith's Six-O-Tine for lost manhood and exhausted nervous system. Makes old young and vigorous — a powerful brain food and nerve stimulant," the full page advertisement related. And all for only 50 cents!

One of the first methods used by Walter to create a market for his new drink was to employ the 1904 equivalent of today's "forced demand." He would patronize Schimpf's, Klosky's or other better restaurants of the era, ask for Coca-Cola and then decline to dine there if the drink were unavailable. He encouraged newly-made acquaintenances to take the same action; and to demonstrate to some proprietors the popularity of the drink, he would down three or four at a sitting and virtually flow out the door upon his departure.

In his sales efforts, Walter worked hard to sell one particularly burly saloon keeper who resisted sales pressure with equal force, threatening to "throw him out if he came in one more time." Walter called on Will, who owned half of the Mobile business, for assistance. When he was next in Mobile, Will took one look at the sales prospect and told Walter:

"You tend to your own fights, I'm going back to Montgomery."

12

WHILE WALTER was growing intellectually and broadening his interests, he was reaching the halfway mark of man's three score and ten. About six feet one in height, he remained slight in build but had filled out sufficiently to offset the prominence of his facial extremities. He jokingly remarked that "since acorn time is setting in, I am getting fat, am so stout that I can hardly stoop over to button my shoes. The last seven weeks, I have gained one pound and seven ounces [according to his plant's scales, no doubt] and from present indications, I will gain one pound more before Christmas."

In addition to being trim, Walter Bellingrath dressed as neatly and attractively as his income would permit. His features were irregular, but he was by no means an unhandsome man — dark-haired, ruddy-skinned — as he was seen making his sales calls about the city, visiting a saloon now and then and attending church.

Walter's perseverance, long hours and effective salesmanship during his first two years in the bottling business began to pay dividends. It enabled him to see some silver, not just clouds. He proudly related that during the month of May, 1905, his company had sold an average of 30 shipping cases per day, sent via rail and river, and his wagon delivered an average of 62 city cases per day. His gross revenue per 24-bottle case at that time was 75 cents.

Whether it was overwork, overplay or both, Walter became conscious of his health and concerned about an "indisposition" that had been bothering him for months. He consulted a physician who prescribed some medicine "that has done me a great deal of good . . . if I continue to improve I will certainly be fine in another month."

But Walter's forecast was inaccurate, for he and Brother Will were off only a few months later to the Majestic Hotel and Bath House at Hot Springs, Arkansas. There he passed the time reading, writing letters, taking long walks and enjoying the "hot and cold water and telephone service in every room," as advertised by the hotel.

With a knowing twinkle in his eye, he reported that "from the temperature of some of the springs here, one would think Hell fire and brimstone were pretty close by."

13

WALTER BELLINGRATH may have thought the devil was close on his heels, but actually the pursuer was a boy, not a man, armed with drawn bow rather than pitchfork.

The first arrow from the bow struck his brother, Will, and while they were enjoying the lassitude of Hot Springs, Walter heard him express many an idyl of love for a young lady named Mary Nesbitt Elmore. Probably with misty memories of Bethulia, Walter was moved by his brother's love for Mary and wrote to his mother:

"I certainly hope she will prove the companion and wife he thinks she will. Wouldn't see that boy disappointed in marriage for my right arm. I do believe it would hurt me to have it as bad as he's got it . . . one ecstatic feeling after another would chase themselves up and down in me until I'm afraid they would tickle me to death."

Within a few months after writing those lines, Walter began to see his stenographer in a different light from when he had hired her to assist him with his correspondence and other details of running the bottling company. He began to equate her sense of organization and efficiency in personal terms, and his admiration of her professionalism began to assume a pleasing new aspect.

He became aware also of her pleasant face and deep blue eyes topped by a full crown of dark hair, and her youthful vitality. Nearly a foot shorter than Walter, her cinched waist accentuated the rounded hips and full bosom under her office uniform: a starched white blouse with slightly puffed shoulders and high neck collar encircled by a narrow black ribbon tie. Her dark, floor length skirt swished musically as she

Walter and his wife/secretary, Bessie, at a bottling plant occupied a few years after the 1906 storm

moved about the small office and occasionally and accidentally brushed against her employer. Her proximity and well-scrubbed scent triggered the same sensations Walter had earlier thought reserved for lovesick Will.

His day-to-day association with his stenographer and his regard for her intelligence and feminine gentleness, injected her prominently into Walter's reveries. He was timorous and hesitant, however, about disturbing the smooth functioning office relationship and was uncertain of her true feelings for him. This uncertainty was allayed when he received by mail a watch fob locket then given with propriety by young ladies of the day to their gentlemen friends.

Walter at first thought the locket had come from a lady friend in Montgomery. But he was delighted to learn it had been sent by his stenographer. He soon decided to settle down at the age of 35 and enlist the aid of a wife in his avowed battle against the devil.

Bessie Mae Morse was a pioneer stenographer, a liberated feminist of her day with courage to kick tradition and invade the male business world. Her family was of modest means (her father was a shipwright), but her heritage was good New England stock. Their home was not among the imposing residences of the downtown city, but was a neat though un-prepossessing house near the western limit of the city on north Lafayette Street.

Miss Bessie had fallen in love with the boss, found her daily relationship with him to be a happy one, and unhesitantly accepted Walter's proposal of marriage. As for Walter, his love for "Miss Bessie" manifestly was deeper and more serious than the affection he had experienced during his younger days. His attitude toward his pending marriage was a serious one, but his solemnity was mitigated by the usual lighthearted thoughts of bridegrooms-to-be. He wrote his mother about a month before his wedding:

> Now that I am about to take a wife, I sincerely hope and pray that henceforth she and I will be as Godfearing and steadfast a couple as you and papa were. So far I have failed to measure up to the example you and he set, but from now on I earnestly pray God to help me to be all that you all were and even more, if possible.

New and old forms of transportation at the curb of Mr. Bell's plant about 1911. This building, with additions, served as the bottling company's headquarters until 1975.

Well, my time of singleness is fast approaching an end. So far I have not become nervous but suppose when the time comes I will not prove an exception to the rule. Bess doesn't seem to be nervous either, but I am quite sure she will join me in the shakes on our wedding day.

There would be numerous unfilled seats at Walter's and Bessie's wedding, ones which would have been occupied by deceased friends and family members who could not wait for Walter Bellingrath's late marriage. His father, an older brother and sister and Uncle Albert were dead, and Miss Lilly could not attend. But, in writing of his plans for housing other family members and friends, Walter said he wanted "you all to come down a few days ahead of time so I can sort of get use to having a woman or so around sitting on my shirt tail occasionally before I take that leap, after which I'll have one of my own to sit on it, who I believe is going to refuse any other lady that privilege. . . ."

The date for the marriage of Walter Duncan Bellingrath and Bessie Mae Morse was set for November 14, 1906, with the wedding to be held at the Morse home. It was a date almost not kept because of the disastrous hurricane in September of that year. His plant was put out of business for several days by high water, a partially wrecked roof and loss of shipping cases and bottles in coastal towns deluged by high water. Even the riverboat *Mary,* which he occasionally used for shipment of his bottled drinks, was destroyed by the wind's force as it was driven onto a wharf not far from Walter's plant.

Walter, who once expressed his fear of wind when a storm hit nearby when he lived in Jasper, said after the Mobile hurricane that the next time they hang out "that weather flag, I'm going to leave town." But, despite his anxiety, Walter's losses were relatively light, and he luckily was not put out of business. He still had the financial ability to support a wife, and the wedding was held on schedule.

For the first time in nearly 15 years, Walter escaped the confinement and loneliness of rooming house celibacy. He and his bride, after a wedding trip to Niagara Falls, moved into a rented yellow and brown raised cottage on St. Anthony Street, only a short distance from the new larger plant he bought after the hurricane, where he and Bessie would daily make the transformation from carefree bride and groom to hardworking Girl Friday and Boss.

14

ISOLATED from the U. S. mainstream as it was in the early 1900's Mobile sought to maintain its cosmopolitan air with gaiety and divertissements independent of outside stimuli. The social establishment of the city was deep into mystic societies and Mardi Gras, with its flamboyant street parades, gala balls and private parties. Others looked to fraternal organizations and comparable togetherness for relief from the routine of provincialism.

Bell and Bess, as he privately referred to themselves at this time, apparently cared little for Mobile's social scene and made no effort to penetrate its forbidding bastion. They found enjoyment in building the Mobile Coca-Cola Company and in occasional travel. Should he sometimes be absent, Bess was at the office to make certain Coca-Cola flowed copiously and directly to its destinations. They made a good team, and with a nervous system demanding little sleep, Walter worked long hours and sometimes slept only four or five when the workload necessitated it.

Walter Bellingrath was an astute business man, and he continued to overcome the prejudice against Coca-Cola and to dispel the myths concerning its ingredients. He became almost paranoid on the subject and reportedly resigned from one church because of congregational whisperings that he was peddling "dope". Much of his early advertising budget was directed against rumor mongers. Of the flyers he circulated among dealers, one contained testimonials from "eminent chemists" and asserted in bold display type:

These and many other eminent chemists agree that Coca-Cola is Absolutely Harmless but is Genuinely Good to the

Business office and personnel of the Mobile Coca-Cola Bottling Company in 1912. Mr. Bellingrath is in the background doorway.

taste and an aid to Digestion. Hundreds of thousands of dollars are being Spent in Advertising. People Want Coca-Cola. They will go to your Store if you handle the Genuine Coca-Cola The Great National Food Drink."

The pamphlet told also why the War Department had revoked its order against the sale of Coca-Cola at Army post exchanges after no cocaine or alcohol was found in an analysis made by the Department of Agriculture.

Thirty-one years after Walter Bellingrath entered the bottling business at Mobile, he vividly and humorously recounted, in an address delivered to a bottlers' convention in 1934, what it was like to do business as a pioneer:

> . . .eggs were three dozen for 25¢; butter 10¢ a pound, milk 5¢ a quart; the butcher gave away liver and treated the kids to bologna; the hired girl received $2.00 a week and did the washing; women did not powder and paint (in public), smoke, vote, play bridge, strip poker or drink; men wore whiskers and boots, chewed tobacco, spit on the sidewalk and cussed; beer was 5¢ and the lunch free; laborers worked ten hours a day and never went on a strike; no tips were given to waiters and the hat-check graft was unknown; a kerosene hanging lamp and a stereoscope in the parlor were luxuries; no one was ever operated on for appendicitis, or bought glands — microbes and halitosis were unheard of; folks lived to a good old age and every year walked miles to wish their friends MERRY CHRISTMAS.
>
> . . . (we) bottled seltzer water in quart bottles as a side line, for the reason that 90% or more of the customers. . . at that time, and for many years thereafter, operated a combination grocery and saloon or straight saloon. Many of them required seltzer water to make the old time famous whiskey high ball.

As additional proof that payola and kickbacks did not originate in the mid-twentieth century, Bellingrath's speech recalled:

> It had been a long established custom for the route salesmen to partly barter their soft drinks in exchange for hard drinks, when making sales . . . the route salesman was expected to spend not less than 10¢ and sometimes as much as 25¢ on every case the dealer bought for 75¢. Most often this trade back money was spent buying the barkeeper and

A Thanksgiving reunion in Montgomery in 1921, showing Mrs. Leonard Bellingrath, center, and five surviving children of her original eight. Walter is center foreground. Others are, left to right, Leonard, Maude (Mrs. John S. Burnett), Mrs. Bellingrath, Kate (Mrs. W.N. Brown), and Will.

the loiterers around the bar drinks . . . while in other instances the trade back money was passed back to the dealer in cash.

It was then a common practice of route salesmen to give from two to six bottles as a "nap" with nearly every case they sold. This abuse was especially practiced when the customers' business was conducted in a "three-in-one" combination building, embracing a home, grocery and bar room, the salesman always claiming the extras were . . . for the dealer's children.

Despite the business "freebies" of the era, the Mobile Coca-Cola Company continued to prosper and by 1908, Walter and Will had divided their territories, Walt taking Mobile and his brother, Montgomery. There was no friction or misunderstanding or either side. They simply agreed to separate their business affairs.

A genuine sentimentalist whose eyes often misted with emotion, Walter expressed his brotherly love for Will shortly before the latter was to be married.

Excerpts from a long letter said:

> Yes, Billie, you and I have been exceptional brothers, for truly we have been comrades ever since we were boys . . . Often when I am left alone with my thoughts . . . I feel like imploring "Old Father Time" to turn back in his flight and and make us children again for a night. If such a thing were possible, I think I could sit and hold the calf off, or hold Daisy's tail, to keep her from switching you in the face . . . But all these things are now in the forever past, and . . . in order to keep off the melancholy days that come, feed our souls on the very present hope that tomorrow will be better than today.
>
> For instance, you are to soon latch on to a new bed fellow, and I hope she will prove to be as congenial and as sympathetic companion, and true friend and brother to you that I have endeavored to be from my cradle to this stage of the game. Billie, if you don't know I love you, there is nothing I can say to convince you that I do . . . of all men you appear to me as one of the noblest.

And then with superb timing in knowing when to switch to laughter, Walter added: "But what has the foregoing to do with the kind of breeches I am going to wear to your wedding.

Well! I will assure you in advance that they will not be bed-ticking, but something that will harmonize with the sample you sent me.''

Walter's filial thoughts were not confined to Will. There were four other Bellingrath siblings who were prominent in the mind of their brother. Despite his preoccupation with his Mobile company, Walter Bellingrath, along with Brother Will, had by 1910 helped established a Bellingrath Coca-Cola dynasty extending from Alabama into Arkansas.

Sister Kate and her husband, W. N. Brown, had the Selma bottling franchise; Sister Mary Elizabeth (Mamie) and her husband, J. S. Burnett, had Andalusia, Alabama, as their territory; Theodore Leon, married to Miss Maude Smith, was in Little Rock, and Leonard Ferdinand, married to Miss Janie Castleberry, ran the Pine Bluff plant.

All became successful in their businesses, but Walter and Will often were called upon for advice and trouble-shooting to help brothers and sisters to overcome their early business perplexities.

For his family and himself, Walter Bellingrath had accomplished a great deal during his first seven years in Mobile. They were difficult years with more than their share of financial worries. But that was all behind him as his career moved into 1911 and as his initial dislike for the city was forgotten. He had long since hired a new stenographer but enjoyed the love, companionship and influence of the same wife. Walter was in his 41st year, and life for him was beginning to open new vistas, some brightened by success, others shadowed by personal shortcomings.

15

AFTER THE DEATH of an old and beloved friend of his, Walter Bellingrath reflected on the sunshine of her life, and of "the ever present thought of how much more sunshine and how many less shadows I might make on my journey to my inevitable end."

There was to be both light and darkness during the first decade of affluence enjoyed by Walt and Bessie. As his business prospered, and his reputation made itself felt in financial circles, the Bellingrath couple began to reach for new creature comforts and other pleasures. Of particular joy to them was the house they purchased and occupied late in 1911. The city was then moving westward, and Walt and Bessie moved with it to a large three-story house on South Ann Street. It was almost new, having been built less than three years previously.

The new home was considered by Walter to be in the best neighborhood in Mobile, and his interest in natural beauty was rekindled by the spacious grounds of the house, its garden area and large oak and pecan trees. His love of the outdoors, born during his years in Castleberry, had been latent but again was expressed in enthusiasm for his move to a wooded, less crowded part of the city.

As for Bessie Bellingrath, she now realized the paramount wish of most women: not only a grand home of her own but a strong desire to furnish it handsomely and the means with which to do so. The Bellingrath union, during its five years, had not produced children. Walter found his work compensation for the absence of little ones in his life, but Bessie was no doubt bored and sometimes lonely. She no longer worked, had no active social life and was hungry for an interest other than homemaking. Now she found it. Her interest in dealing with tradespeople and acquiring beautiful furniture, silver and objets d'art was one she enjoyed throughout her life and would make itself felt on countless other people.

The newly acquired Bellingrath property ran in depth from one street to the next, and both Walter and his wife eventually developed it into a colorful azalea garden. It annually attracted the admiration of many Mobilians as they walked or drove through the property in the increasing numbers of touring cars seen in the city.

The decade before the Twenties was a time of happiness for Walter that overshadowed occasional self-doubts. The Ann Street home was within easy walking distance of the recently built Central Presbyterian Church, which he vowed to attend regularly. He did, and even became a deacon of that church. Walter's belief in the Lord and faith in his power to turn aside temptation were unquestionably sincere and oft-expressed. But he sometimes felt that he and the Lord were in the loser's corner.

Some of the advertised whiskies of the day were Fisherman's Delight, King Edward Rye, Belle of Mobile and Big Hit. While his preference is not known, whatever his choice, the mere fact that Walter tended to drift with the crowd during this pleasure-seeking era was a source of concern to him.

But there was no "drifting" from his fidelity to Bessie. Walter admired attractive women as fervently as the next man, and an added sparkle in his eyes usually signalled the approach of one. However, his was an attitude of look, not handle. It was more kittenish than tom-cattish, and his ego would soar when inflated by the attention of pretty, young coquettes of the era. This appreciation of feminine charms is best described by two episodes that occurred many years later in Walter's life. When he was about 70, Mr. Bellingrath was asked how old a man had to be before he stopped noticing attractive women.

"I don't know," was the reply. "Ask him," his 90-year-old father-in-law, Mr. Morse.

And in 1951, shortly after Miss Yolande Betbeze of Mobile

was chosen Miss America, a friend of Mr. Bellingrath suggested, to help publicize the area's floral beauty, he send her flowers during one of her personal appearances in a northern city. After meeting Miss America several months later, Mr. Bell asked his friend if the flowers had been sent and how many.

"Only sixteen dollars worth," he exclaimed. "If I'd known she was that beautiful, I'd have spent a hundred."

In 1912, Walter's frivolous interest in the ladies was dimmed by concern for his health.

He at first planned to take his private physician with him to French Lick Springs but decided against it. On arrival at the hotel of the same name, he put his fate in the hands of a spa physician and natural Pluto water. The treatment helped him, and his health promptly improved.

The Indiana spa offered Walt and Bess their first exposure to the pre-war jet set, the so-called Robber Barons of the period. He was impressed by the Vanderbilts, the Harrimans, the Gateses, their millions, their private cars and by the daring dress of some women members of the wealthy group. The decollete dresses caused one man to remark to Walter that "he had seen things he had not seen since he was weaned."

Walter was only momentarily diverted by jewels, expensive gowns and partially bared breasts. He was concerned, according to his letters, about his brother's Coca-Cola operation in Little Rock and other personal and business matters. He manifested pleasure, however, in his new strength of character and resultant abstinence. He wrote his mother that "I don't feel like the Pharisee did when he stood up and thanked God he was not like other people, but I do feel and act like Blind Tom used to do when he played the piano. You know he always, after playing a piece, stood up and applauded himself when the audience applauded."

Walter added that he frequently applauded himself in secret when there was no audience.

The devoted son was then 45; his mother, confined to a wheel chair, was four score.

16

THE MORAL and spiritual goals Walter Bellingrath had set for himself continued to be elusive, but the frequent struggles with his conscience began to produce noticeable results. On Mother's Day, 1916, he informed his mother that "I have not turned your hand loose for one moment since I took hold of it the 17th of last October, and by the grace of God, I do not intend to ever let it go again."

Mother's Day in Mobile, and the rest of the nation, was then celebrated with many outpourings of sentiment. There was less commercialism and more church services, flags and proclamations from the President of the U.S. down to the city's mayor. Motormen on Mobile's trolleys not only sported company-furnished carnations but stopped their cars at noon for three minutes as a tribute to mothers of the world.

Walter's tribute to Catherine Jean Bellingrath occupied nearly six pages of flowery prose. Prior to the reference to taking his mother's hand, he declared: "Others may have been blessed with more wealth and worldly goods, but none were ever blessed with purer, Godlier or better parents than we your children. And as day after day of the evening of your life slip past, may God grant that each of us prove a greater blessing to you and our fellow man is my earnest prayer."

Enclosed with the letter was a reprint of one of the songs he and Bess had sung at church on Mother's Day. It was entitled, "My Mother 'Tis of Thee," sung, of course, to the tune of "America."

Mother's Day commercialism may not have been prevalent in 1916, but Walt was in there fighting in keep the name Coca-Cola as repected and unsullied as motherhood. The entire backs of his company envelopes were printed with an advertising message directed at "serpents in the garden", as *Fortune* magazine years later would describe the imitators of Coca-Cola. Walter Bellingrath's envelope advertisement asked: "IS IT A CRIME TO SUBSTITUTE?" After about 250 words of heady copy, the message concluded: "SUBSTITUTES are a LIBEL on the HONEST MANUFACTURER. CALL FOR IT BY NAME. Demand and see that you get genuine bottled COCA-COLA. Refuse substitutes."

Aggressive marketing methods paid off for Walter, and his company continued to expand and add to his material resources. Not only did he acquire contiguous property for his plant, including livery stables, but Walter's new prosperity was evident in monetary gifts to his mother and other relatives on birthdays and Christmases. The $2.50 Christmas gift belatedly sent from Jasper was replaced by gifts of ten and twenty-five dollars.

Success for Walter soon became proliferous. New business opportunities began to arise, and in one of them the interest of the father was shared by the son. Walter had not inherited his father's creative or technical skills, but he had been sufficiently exposed to the turpentine industry to be aware of its potential in the rich pine forests of the deep south.

His chance to enter the naval stores field, in an ancillary way, came in the person of Louis J. Lerio, who came to Mobile at the beginning of the century as a northern transplant. He was a master metal craftsman, as was Bellingrath's father. By 1910, Lerio had become involved in the naval stores industry and was using his inventive capabilities to design tools and equipment for turpentine producers. He found a method of creating a sheet metal cup to replace the clay "cup and gutter" system, then used to extract raw pine rosin from the trees.

To help get the metal cup on the market, Bellingrath in 1913 provided the financial assistance and business knowledge to form the Lerio Patent Cup Company. The company grew, prospered and diversified its manufactured products. Bellingrath became president of the company, following the death of Mr. Lerio in 1942 and chairman of the board a few years before his own death.

Walter's association with the Lerio company always gave

him "melancholy pleasure" — to use one of his favorite phrases. He again was close to the naval stores industry and occasionally discovered, to his elation, he was doing business with men who had known his father.

The sweetness of Walter's success in his bottling and manufacturing businesses soon was soured by the adversity of another hurricane. It struck on July 5, 1916, with little advance warning, and late in the afternoon the wind shifted from northeast to south and piled much of the waters of Mobile Bay into low-lying areas of the city. According to Walter, the water reached a four-foot depth in the Coca-Cola plant and nearly five in the turpentine cup factory. This led Walter to believe that Mobile was a "Jonah place" for him, a city of catastrophes.

In 1905, he had seen a raging fire, a threatening distance from his first plant, destroy the community's principal hotel, The Battle House; and a year later his own business was nearly swept into the river and bay. "I was hurt and am still wounded," He said of the 1916 storm. "I have begun to feel that . . . just as fast as I come from under one disaster another one overtakes me." He reported a heavy loss of cases and bottles both in Mobile and at river landings, in addition to in-plant damage at both of his companies.

The Bellingrath home, its roof under repair at the time, also was damaged considerably. The ceilings of four rooms fell as a result of the leaking roof.

It was no wonder, a month later, Walter Bellingrath contemplated the devil and his own chagrin. He reasoned that people of strong moral character were not only on the Lord's side but "had Him and kept Him when the tempter showed up, while poor me had gone astray and wandered over onto the Devil's premises. And then when he came around I immediately got into a dispute with him as to whether it was he or I that was legally monarch of his own premises. As a consequence, I, of course, always got whipped."

By this time, Walter was taking a more active interest in civic life in the community, and his contributions culminated with his election in 1917 as president of the Mobile Chamber of Commerce and Business League. The U. S. was at war with Germany; Walter was only one generation removed from the Rhineland. These related facts doubled his gratification over the trust members of the business organization placed in him at a time when almost anything German was cause for suspicion.

As the war wore on, Walter became increasingly philosophical about it. He once said he would be unfaithful to his father's memory if he did not emphasize that "I do not believe it is the German people who are responsible for this horrible war but . . . by their military rulers. I cannot believe the American people bear the true German citizen malice, and they would be accepted into the sisterhood of republics of the world, if they would only overthrow forever the delirious military power and authority and achieve control of their own affairs.

". . . I pray God the whole bloody struggle may soon end, and with its ending, war as a means of settling differences will forever be banished from the face of the earth."

In referring to other instances of might being substituted for right, Walter waved his colors as a loyal southerner and unreconstructed rebel by citing the North's settlement of the Missouri Compromise question. He criticized also the action of Theodore Roosevelt "when he, by the rule of arbitration and might, swiped the Panama Canal. . . ."

Nevertheless, Mr. Bellingrath's Chamber of Commerce capitalized on the young canal by displaying on its letterhead, "Mobile Gateway to Panama," along with a sketch showing the port on a direct line with the isthmus.

One of the high priority projects of Walter Bellingrath's reign as president of the Chamber was to have Mobile included on a military highway extending from Bangor to Seattle, connecting fortified positions along the three coasts and the Mexican border. It was to be part of the national defense of the nation.

The Mobile Chamber was going all out to help save the country by repelling the Hun or any other invader; but the bulletin also noted, in familiar Chamber of Commerce style, that the success of the effort probably would mean a much needed road to an adjacent county and a better road from Mobile to New Orleans.

Most of his fellowmen saw Walter Bellingrath differently from the way he saw himself. He was not found wanting in their eyes, and public tribute was accorded him at the close of 1917 for his leadership in the business and public affairs of Mobile. It was a notable event in Walter's life. He experienced what comes to few men, the greatness and exaltation of tremendous pride.

The tribute was understandably food for his spirit and incentive, and he proudly and privately told his mother about the annual meeting, a banquet of the Mobile Chamber of Commerce.

"It was freely admitted by all that it was the largest, most enthusiastic and most successful public dinner ever staged in Mobile. I was the presiding officer, and when I stood to call the meeting to order, that splendid body of men," he wrote for his mother's pleasure only, "representing the business brains and culture of our city, stood up as one man and applauded me before I had a chance to utter a word. I was so astonished and surprised I came near losing my bearings."

Setting a precedent, Walter was reelected for a second term, and other correspondence of the period asserted he had almost single-handedly guided the business organization through the troubled times of the war. One prominent attorney said that "by his ability, perseverance and integrity he has built himself up to the point of being one of the foremost citizens of our community. In addition to his own personal affairs, he, as president of our Chamber of Commerce, put that organization on a firm foundation and in good standing, when as a matter of fact, when he assumed the position of president, it amounted to naught ... his work has been recognized and appreciated by all as being very valuable."

Shortly before 1920, Walter Bellingrath extended his influence beyond soft drinks and forest products to an unusual corner of the building industry. He acquired financial control of Mobile Ornamental Tile Company. The plant was staffed by numerous Spanish artisans, and many thousands of cement, hand-made tiles, often of custom design, were shipped throughout the U.S. to ornament the Mediterranean-style structures in vogue during the 20's. The floors and walls of several public and private buildings in Mobile, New Orleans, and other cities still display these handsome reminders of the Bellingrath business diversity.

Still casting about for other business opportunities, Walter Bellingrath looked to the sea. He and several other Mobilians met regularly to discuss formation of a steamship line.

At least two of the men "thought big" and would be described today as big spenders. An incident at an organizational meeting, held at the city's leading downtown club, attested to the extravagance of one of them. Noticing that his usual waiter had not served him in several days, he asked the servant why, and remarked:

"I don't understand it, Glover. Haven't I always tipped you most handsomely?"

"Yassuh, but I lost you last week in a crap game."

The company began business in November, 1919, operating a single ship leased to it by the United States Shipping Board. Shortly after incorporation of the company, three additional steamers were obtained. Walter's associates continued to spend money in ways incompatible with his frugality and contrary to the lessons in thrift he had learned while working on the railroad. He later sold his 33 percent of the stock for $1,000. The final straw, it was reported subsequently in financial circles, was a $5 tip to a Pullman porter made by John B. Waterman and entered on one of his Washington expense accounts.

Walter Bellingrath's erroneous judgement of the business ability of the free spenders was one of the most costly business mistakes he ever made. The company grew into the Waterman Steamship Corporation. It operated more ships during World War II than any other U. S. flag line and produced millions for many stockholders who had more confidence than the founder.

17

AS INTERESTED as he was in business during this period of his life, Walter and Bessie found time to harvest and enjoy the rich results of his enterprise.

They traveled together on occasion, visiting their favorite spa and then going on to larger cities. Numerous family holidays were enjoyed together. Walter's mother and brothers and sisters visited the Bellingraths' Mobile home and Walt and Bessie often entrained for a reunion in Montgomery. Walter occasionally visited the parent Coca-Cola company in Atlanta and made enduring friendships among its hierarchy.

But Walter found his greatest, most relaxing pleasure in escaping for a day or two in Mobile's plentiful marshlands. Usually, he and Frank Woodward, his constant fishing companion, guide and paddler, would journey to a placid estuary identified on original French maps as Riviere du Poule. As he cast his lure in the shadows of overhanging bay magnolias, swamp maples, oaks and pines, interspersed with clumps of palmetto bordered by a band of cattails and other marsh grasses, Walter felt certain that this was the most beautiful place in the world.

He and his paddler would fish nearly all day. When they became weary, it was a time for a Coca-Cola. Frank would head for the landing of a dilapidated store run by a Creole family of the area. Or they would escape the midday heat under the mossy boughs of one of many live oaks along the river banks.

As best he could remember, Frank Woodward first paddled Mr. Bell in 1911. Frank, in his words, was a "colored man," not a Creole, and was an unforgettable character in his devotion and faithfulness to the boss. Some said he was Walter Bellingrath's "yes man." But not in a servile way. His sense of humor was as pronounced as his employer's, his happiness effervescent with chuckles and his smile originated in his heart, not his head.

Frank always delighted in descriptively increasing the size of fish caught by Mr. Bell, and often embroidered tales of their experiences on the river: of storm elements, strange fish, and of a sea serpent that blocked the path of their skiff.

"How'd you get by that serpent?" he was asked.

"Oh, he jest dipped in the middle . . . let me paddle across."

Frank told the story also of the time Mr. Bell was fishing with friends. A hawk was seen far away in a tree, and someone wagered Mr. Bellingrath he couldn't hit it. With that challenge, he raised his rifle, took aim, fired. Down came the hawk, with a bullet hole between the eyes.

Frank said the hole was a little jagged because Mr. Bell was standing in a boat vibrating slightly from the running motor. There was no protest from Mr. Bellingrath, who pointed out that both he and Frank were deacons in their respective churches and had implicit confidence in each other's veracity.

Once, for some reason or other, Mr. Bellingrath told Frank Woodward he was fired from his job as Fowl River fishing guide. Frank's reaction was:

"You can't fire me, Mr. Bell."

"And why not, you old rascal?"

"Cause I was here first," was Frank's quick reply.

That disagreement ended in laughter and forgiveness, and Frank Woodward continued to be the outdoor companion of Walter Bellingrath.

Walter occasionally withdrew from marshy solitude, broken only by the swish of Frank's paddle and the cry of a bird or animal, for more gregarious, social, salt-water fishing trips. These usually were out of Coden or Bayou la Batre, at the southern end of Mobile County. It was a way to have pleasant visits with his out-of-town friends, brothers and sisters.

While Walter Bellingrath was fishing, Bessie continued her hunting — for furniture, porcelain, silver and other collectibles. She spent not only her own time in this quest; she relied also on friends among antique dealers to help her locate various treasures, as well as lesser items appealing to her tastes, throughout the Gulf States area. Collecting and associating with people from whom she bought kept Bessie busy. It gave her extreme pleasure, and, if she desired a certain piece, she was never known to haggle. Conversely, in buying from families low on luck, Bessie Bellingrath was known often to pay more than the table or chair was worth. She was particularly well-known for this during the later depression years when many old Southern families were happy to convert mahogany or china into cash.

Mrs. Bellingrath also bought giant azaleas for her Ann Street gardens. One Alabama businessman credited his first year of college to the azaleas she bought from his mother. By the time the Bellingraths were ready to make their move to another residence, their Ann Street house was filled to overflowing with acquisitions that would become increasingly valuable through the years.

While the 1920's were pleasurable and financially successful for Walt and Bessie, the erosion of passing years brought sorrow and heartbreak to the Bellingrath clan. Catherine Jean Bellingrath, Walter's mother, had lived too long. She now faced the death of the third of her eight children.

Theodore Leon Bellingrath, who was born in Cuthbert, Georgia, rather than Atlanta, because his mother fled to escape the ravages of General Sherman, had an equally eventful life. His ups and downs were numerous, and Walter occasionally wrote to his mother about his concern for Thede's future. But Thede had made it over the top in Little Rock, was happily married with children, only to become gravely ill shortly after his 55th birthday.

Walter was saddened, of course, by the threatened loss of one for whom he had shown almost paternal affection; but his anxiety really was for the effect death might have on his mother. After being in Little Rock with nearly all of his brothers and sisters to help Maude Bellingrath and the children, he wrote to his mother:

"I know this grief is coming doubly hard on you. There is little consolation I can offer except the consolation that comes from the throne of Grace and the thought and knowledge that after all He had been good to us as compared to the fateful

69

dispensation he had made of others and the families of others
. . . I am writing to reassure you just how deeply and sincerely
my own heart is sympathizing with you during the distressing
hours and days."

Thede's balance between life and death fluctuated
suspensefully for six weeks or more, with Walter, Will, or Len
answering Maude's appeals for help. But their mother needed
no mortal support. At the age of 85, her religious strength
quieted the swells of her sorrow.

"The last letter you wrote me," Walter acknowledged, "was
one of the most reassuring and beautiful from a real
Christian's standpoint I ever read. If at your age you can so
completely and with such abiding faith and reassurance recon-
cile the vicissitudes and afflictions of this life to the Will of
God, resigning your loved ones and their fate to His will, how
much more eagerly should those of us left accept His grace and
yours."

Thede died a day or two after those words were written.
Walter immediately composed a six-page graphic word picture
of the funeral to the mother who remained in Selma with her in-
firmities, her memories, and His spiritual sustenance.

18

ABOUT 100 YEARS before Walter Bellingrath's forebears fled Germany for the United States, a Frenchman of the lesser nobility responded to the attractions of the New World. A quest for riches and adventure brought him to Mobile, as it had more important Frenchmen: Bienville, d'Iberville, Cadillac, Tonti and others.

Few grants and deeds of the early French period in Mobile have been preserved, but more are available, particularly town lot deeds, from the middle period after 1733. As it became apparent that West Florida, which included Mobile, would be ceded to the British in early 1763, a number of land certificates were issued and have been preserved. These were papers substantiating long occupancy of property and ratification of claims rather than original grants.

Among these recorded certificates is the translation of a petition by Chevalier Montaut de Monberault, dated January 3, 1763, to confirm his possession of a tract of land up Fowl River in a cul-de-sac or turn called Lisloy (Goose Island), where he lived. Boundaries were not given, but the land is believed to have fronted on the Isle-aux-Oies River, the name of the northwest confluent of Fowl River.

Monberault had developed the property as the Lisloy plantation. He used it primarily to raise cattle originally boated from Cuba to Isle Dauphine, only a few miles to south, and brought to the mainland aboard shallow draft lighters. The property was 20 miles or more south of the French fort and settlement at Mobile but was important, along with the rest of the area known as Mon Luis Island, because of its proximity to the port at Isle Dauphine. The island port was used before a channel was cut into Mobile Bay.

Monberault had purchased the land from a Mr. Petit, who obtained it from a Mr. Dauriscourt by way of a man named Lalime, the first settler. None had a title from the government.

"Your petitioner," said Monberault, "finds himself in the same situation with the greater part of the inhabitants of this part of the country, who, in fact, have no other titles to the lands which they occupy than the very incomplete and insufficient right which arises from possession."

The French governor in New Orleans considered the petition and granted the tract to Monberault. He officially got his land before the British formally took over the territory. With other Frenchmen, he was given 18 months in which to renounce his religion and swear allegiance to Great Britain. The alternative was to settle his affairs and leave. He served the British for awhile but was unwilling to surrender his Catholicism. After several unpleasant incidents, he was forced to dispose of the plantation on July 9, 1765, and left with his family for New Orleans.

The property changed hands several times under the English and reverted to lush jungle, until Mobile came under Spanish rule from 1780 to 1813. Peter J. Hamilton, the principal historian of Mobile during colonial days, wrote in 1897 that a former owner of the Lisloy property "had been succeeded before August of 1785 by our second Spanish Governor, Pedro Favrot. This was possibly the beautiful place now known as Parker's, whose oak seventeen feet in circumference has a spread of over one hundred feet. There still exists an irregular enclosure, possibly for cattle or a bull-fight, surrounded by an earthen wall, and pieces of a cement floor are dug up near the fine bluff."

It is this quotation that has given credence through the years to the legend of the Royal Herdsman of Spain raising bulls on the property for shipment to Dauphin Island and thence to bull rings of Spain and Mexico. The Spanish occupants also reportedly planted a lane of live oaks and magnolias, with the Parker oak the only remaining stanchion of an erstwhile canopy of evergreen.

Other ghosts swept lightly and provocatively over the paths

of the Monberault-Favrot-Parker place. Many legends have been told of the area, but one of the most titillating is that of the salty brigand, Jean LaFitte. The pirate, who later received a Presidential pardon because of assistance lent Andrew Jackson in the Battle of New Orleans, was a reputed visitor to the Isle-aux-Oies sanctuary after forays against shipping in the Gulf of Mexico. Stories of his visits and the possible location of buried treasure have been handed down from parent to child among the natives of the area, some of whom claim descendancy from LaFitte crew members. Creole legend goes so far as to say the spirit of Jean LaFitte still roams the woods and marshes to protect his buried booty.

Throughout the late 1800's the whine and screech of saw mills disturbed the tranquility of the Parker place. A man Walter Bellingrath met in 1917, Louis J. Nevin, related to him many of the facts and fantasies of the property. In 1891, he had worked for a Captain Fred Ingate, who operated a saw mill there at the time. Other mill operators in the forests of Fowl River included the Parkers.

But the saw mills had long been silenced, and few vestiges of them remained. Up until 1919, Mary Parker, a descendant of Parkers who once owned thousands of acres in the vicinity, lived on a relatively few acres remaining to the family. A dignified, proud and respected matriarch of her Creole family, Mary Parker earned her living by renting boats and cooking for Mobile sportsmen who frequented the nearby Lisloy Club.

It was in late 1918 that Walter Bellingrath stepped permanently into this history-rich, wooded paradise. The land and its waters had challenged the imagination, muscle and ingenuity of many. Some had moderately succeeded, others had failed; the land had not yet met its master and was yet to reach its full potential.

19

AS OFTEN IS TRUE of men and women, it was illness that caused a major turning point in Walter Bellingrath's life. The decisive factor that led to his most substantial and enduring accomplishment was physical frailty, not strength. It was a fortunate paradox.

The effects of influenza, business anxiety over the shortage of sugar and Coca-Cola syrup and the inroads of age considerably weakened Walter toward the end of the World War I. Instead of relying again on the magical powers of mineral waters at a distant resort, Walter consulted his Mobile physician, Dr. P. D. McGehee. He was advised to create his own spa, get out in the country more often, reduce business activities, learn how to play with greater regularity and beyond the pressures of urban life.

Bess, also, had been ill with threatened pneumonia on several occasions, giving additional weight to the doctor's orders. Walter began to look for a suitable retreat, preferably near the water, where he could fish and otherwise relax. A friend and employee knew of the perfect spot, the Lisloy fishing club on the Isle-aux-Oies River, about a mile and a half up Fowl River from its entrance to Mobile Bay.

Having occasionally fished Fowl River with Frank Woodward, Walter was delighted by the prospect of acquiring property on the high, beautiful, wooded site. In late November, 1918, he wrote an old friend in Atlanta: "If a trade I am now negotiating goes through, I expect to acquire 25 acres of land on Fowl River near Coden [Coq d'Inde], on which it is my intention to build a comfortable bungalow to be used as a country resort and fishing grounds and a place to entertain our friends when they come to see us."

Riverfront view of Bell Camp when it was bought by Mr. Bell in early 1919. The left building was rebuilt into the Lodge, and the kitchen house at right was replaced by the Bellingrath Home in 1935-36.

Walter was uncertain whether his offer for the property would be accepted, but he wrote his mother in February, 1919:

"Ma, I have bought me a beautiful site on Fowl River, 21 miles from Mobile. The property has two small real country cottages on it. They are old, but I have fixed them up some, and they are really fine camps. I have temporarily named my camp 'Bell's Camp.' I am thinking of changing the name to 'Bell Camp.' Many of my most intimate friends call me 'Bell' from which is conceived the name . . . Can you suggest a more appropriate name that will at the same time suggest my name? I am dead anxious for you to see my camp and spend a few days there with me. . . ."

Bellingrath soon bought adjoining property from Mary Parker, increasing the size of Bell Camp to 60 acres. A total of three old shacks, built of sturdy pine planks, resting on foundations of unenclosed brick piers, were on the overall property. Mr. Bell intended to put into effect one of the favorite sayings of the Spanish who preceded him on the land: "The days were made for rest, and the nights were made for sleep." But Walter couldn't take it that easy. There was much to be done to rehabilitate the dwellings and clean up wilderness adjoining them.

Making the houses livable, after fumigating and scrubbing, was a challenging chore and an employment opportunity for the male relatives of Mary Parker and other Creoles of the area. And now, the paternalism of Mr. Bell advanced beyond his relationship with Frank, his boatman. He might not pay more than the going rate or otherwise pamper his Creole or "colored" employees in monetary ways, but he was a father figure to them throughout his lifetime. Those close to him warranted his trust and always looked to him for help when it was needed. He asked for two cents change when he gave his driver five cents for three-cent newspaper, but he would altruistically rescue him, or others, from the tentacles of the law or pay burdensome doctors bills.

Mr. Bell may not have been sufficiently skillful to supervise reconstruction of the decaying houses, but there was someone else within the family with necessary qualifications — his father-in-law. He hired S. W. Morse, the shipwright, to supervise the job making one of the buildings into a kitchen and dining room and another into sleeping quarters. The latter cottage became known as the Lodge, and several years later it was enlarged, with a screened porch extending the full length of the building. Mr. Bell let Mary Parker continue to occupy the third house during her lifetime, and it was used later by Hattie Jenkins, the first cook at Bell Camp.

The awesome task of clearing the wilderness also was a challenge to the Bellingrath pocketbook and energy. There was only one open space, evidently used by the Parker family as a vegetable garden, except for clearings adjacent to the houses; but even these areas had nearly returned to jungle by the time the Bellingraths acquired them. The rest of the property, excluding a few paths, was a vine-entangled, almost impenetrable wilderness.

The road leading from the highway, now known as Bellingrath Road, to the entrance of Bell Camp also had to be improved. It was in a deplorable condition and, after heavy rains, almost impassable. Trails inside the camp were better, but they too had to be widened, filled and trimmed of projecting limbs and other foliage.

Despite its remoteness, Bell Camp could be reached by two roads from Mobile, one via the road to New Orleans, and the other to the east across Dog River. Most of the visitors to the area, both before and after its acquisition by Walter Bellingrath, came by buggies and wagons or automobiles. But for those without private means of conveyance, it was possible to reach the Lisloy Club (Parker's Place) by train. At the time there was a small, branch-line railroad, the Bay Shore division of the old Mobile and Ohio, passing within a mile of the property and continuing on to the fishing and resort villages of Coden and Bayou la Batre. Service consisted of one train daily. It arrived at the shedlike "Parker Station" in the afternoon and returned the following morning. On Sundays, however, "The Fisherman's Special" departed Mobile early in the morning and returned late the same day. This passenger service was discontinued in the early 20's, and the tracks later removed for scrap.

Walt and Bessie would never be satisfied with the improvement and beautification of Bell Camp. For them, it was a project without end. However, work had progressed sufficiently by January 1, 1919, to entertain guests at Bell Camp for the first time since the land was acquired.

20

"I BUILT MY CAMP because I wanted a place to lie down with my feet on the sofa."

This reasoning pointedly described the formality of Walter's urban home life. His home was not *his* castle, but Bessie's. While he appreciated the beauty and elegance of the city house, Bell Camp mirrored his personality and heritage. It launched a decade of personal happiness and contentment for Walter Bellingrath, and the prescription of Dr. McGehee was patently filled. The informality of the place, its wooded and watery insulation against city pressures and irritations inspired Walter to become socially more gregarious. Also, it gave him an opportunity to transfer some of his filial affection to members of Bessie's family. Two of Mrs. Bellingrath's nieces returned with their parents from Texas during the '20's. They, along with sons of two other Morse sisters, were frequent visitors to the camp with their friends.

"Little Alice," one of the nieces, was a favorite of Mr. and Mrs. Bellingrath, and occasional Friday night dances, with music courtesy of a hand-cranked Victrola, were held for her in the third floor ballroom of the Ann Street home. It was kind of Bessie, Walter thought, to help bring her nieces out, but such entertainment couldn't hold a candle, in his opinion, to the possibilities for amusement at Bell Camp.

Guests lists, penned in yellowed registration books once used by hotels, attest to the fun-filled days and nights of both adult and adolescent houseparties at Bell Camp.

A pier was built into the Isle-aux-Oies River shortly after the houses were remodeled, and many sunny hours were spent there by young and old alike. Crab lines, chicken-neck bait, nets and fishing equipment were plentiful, as were skiffs for more skilled fishermen who wished to paddle the river and cast along its reed-bordered banks.

On several occasions, Walter was dramatically reminded that boats and danger go hand-in-hand. Once he came close to losing not only his indispensable boatman, Frank Woodward, but also a friend from New Orleans. The pair was fishing when they were startled by a frightening roar becoming progressively louder. Looking in the distance, they saw trees and shrubs being toppled or topped by a small tornado. The usually placid river began to froth, and Frank paddled frantically in what he hoped was the safe direction. It was. The tornado only rocked the boat, as the funnel moved farther inland.

Years later, Lodge guests enjoyed the luxury of one of the first speed boats in the area, an open mahogany one with perpendicular bow and a maximum speed in keeping with the times. Nevertheless, the speed was sufficient to cause it to flip when a steering cable broke. Everyone was accounted for except a little girl. Panic was brief, however, for the boat was immediately righted, and there was the child. Her life jacket had snagged on a cleat, and she was trapped under the boat with her head safely in the air pocket provided by the cockpit.

Those involved thought the Bellingrath temper would erupt over water damage to his boat and motor, but he was so relieved on learning no one was injured, he merely issued orders for the purchase of replacement eye glasses for those lost by Johnnie Dickinson, the Creole skipper of the boat.

It would have taken more than the threat of injury to dampen enthusiasm of those who enjoyed water sports, land games and exploration of the camp's surrounding woods. An added attraction for the young was more Coca-Cola — "Dopes," as they were called by many — than they could possibly drink. When they tired of fishing and crabbing, many boys played baseball in the clearing adjoining historic Parker Oak. Mr. Bell was once in the vicinity when he heard some of the young ones suggest stopping the game for a "Dope."

It nearly was the final visit of the boys to Bell Camp. Mr. Bellingrath called them in the house, lined them up, and gave them a restrained demonstration of his dislike for any one who spoke disparagingly of his liquid livelihood. He found the word "Dope" particularly offensive, since rumors about Coke's ingredients were being circulated by liquor distillers who credited the company with being an influential force behind the Volstead Act.

Mrs. Bellingrath always was on hand as proper chaperone for the mixed houseparties and was careful to bolster all defenses against temptation. An exceptionally proper person, and straightlaced tighter than her corsets, Bessie Bellingrath was offended when the exuberant evangelist, Billy Sunday, playfully slapped Mrs. Sunday on the fanny during a visit to the Bellingrath home. The incident followed a revival meeting in an old cotton warehouse near the Mobile waterfront.

To make certain there was no fanny patting, or petting, among her young guests, Bessie saw to it the woods about the Lodge were well lighted. And when she blinked those lights at 10 o'clock, it was the signal for immediate occupancy by the boys and girls of their well-segregated sleeping quarters. Only one young lady, more amorous or venturesome than the others, regularly eluded Miss Bessie's nocturnal patrol. When another girl discovered her date had rendezvoused in the boat house with her friend, she became so angry she assigned his high school ring to the Isle-aux-Oise along with the elusive treasure of LaFitte.

The lord and master of Bell Camp didn't take life as seriously as its mistress. Despite his years, Walter maintained his boyish zest for teasing the youngsters and playing practical jokes on susceptible guests. One of his favorite tricks was to place a portable Victrola under a bunk in the girls' sleeping quarters. The volume was set at full, and in the morning a maid was sent into the room to start the contraption. All but the heaviest of sleepers would be startled awake with a blast by Sousa or some other rousing number.

It wasn't all adolescent fun and games at the Lodge. Walter reached the age of 50 during his first summer at the camp. Home continued to be Ann Street, but he spent many long weekends at the Lodge with Mobile fishing friends and out-of-town guests. When the Lodge was enlarged to include a giant brick-and-tile fireplace, Walter made certain the mantel was the right height for his elbow. A man of nervous energy, he found standing more rewarding then sitting, and his favorite postprandial position was leaning on the mantel while rhetorically holding the floor against all assailants. Near his elbow was an appropriately engraved silver loving cup given to him by his mother on his 50th birthday. Around his middle was a belt with a gold buckle from Bessie and across it, a watch chain from appreciative in-laws. In this posture and on home territory, Walter delighted in lecturing visiting executives from The Coca-Cola Company in Atlanta. He told them they had preached to him all week; now it was his turn to occupy the catbird seat.

Refreshment at some of these stag occasions — when Miss Bessie wasn't present — was so-called swamp elixir distilled in the nearby woods. It was said Coca-Cola officials helped bring on prohibition, but Walter was hardly among them. He enjoyed the camaraderie of his fishing companions and other visitors. And as a prominent Mobile attorney and close friend of Mr. Bell recalled in jest during a public speech many years later, he and Walter managed "to see some strange snakes" during their outings at the camp. Judge Turner enjoyed a song fest as much as Walter Bellingrath, and strains of spirituals and other old-time songs, with an occasional harmonica cadenza, periodically were heard over the other night sounds.

This type of fellowship was enjoyed by Walter, but he was determined as ever to remain temperate. He would send his "run man," one of his employees, to a nearby bootlegger for a pint at a time. After making several forays into the woods, the servant asked Mr. Bell if he could buy more than a pint.

The frank, unabashed reply was: "Damn it no. I might be tempted to drink it."

21

THE EUPHORIC PLEASURES of Bell Camp were savored continually by the Bellingraths, but the effect was not one of lassitude and inactivity. Their vision and ambition precluded dreamy contentment from displacing energy and initiative. Work at the camp was intensified and accelerated.

Water problems were not the least of Walter Bellingrath's worries. The houses had been improved and modernized, but the water system was basically a bucket brigade between the kitchen and a spring at the river's edge. This was as undesirable as other outdoor plumbing of the day. Efforts were made to divert the water's flow to the houses but without success. Next, a small pond, a reminder of the sawmill's need of fresh water for boilers, was cleaned and a pump installed at one end. The water was pumped to a cistern Bessie's father built, but it could be used only for kitchen and household use. It was not drinkable.

Subsequent drilling efforts produced a plentiful supply of water, but it was heavy with sulphur and salt. This was diverted to a spot where it flowed downward into a marshy area, carving a ravine later to be put to artistic use. Excellent water finally was brought in from a shallower depth at the head of the mill pond.

Little by little, Mr. Bell transformed the marshy mill pond into a lake. Trees were removed, the banks cleared of an entanglement of vines, shrubbery and decayed branches. A new dam was constructed, as was a rustic bridge at the narrow end of the lake, with a trail cut through the jungle to connect the dam with the bridge.

Adjacent to the north end of the mill pond was a narrow bayou, a swampy, undisturbed natural habitat for water fowl, muskrat, beavers and other creatures. This environment welcomed Bell Camp's first pet. An 18-inch alligator was brought to the camp by some of Walter's fishing companions. Each time one of them returned, he would bring a pound or so of liver, strike the water with a paddle and call "Roscoe." The reptile would be fed from a stick, which grew in length with the footage of the alligator. He became so domesticated he would surface the river on command of Frank Woodward to receive a gastronomic reward. Roscoe lived for many years and when last seen was about six feet in length.

The only wildlife — certainly not alligators — of interest to Miss Bessie was the botanical kind. Her city garden had become overcrowded with azaleas and japonicas, as nearly every variety of camellia was then called. The natural displacement area for them was Bell Camp. Neither she nor Walter had any idea of transforming a fishing camp into a garden; but when plants and shrubs were placed about the Lodge, they liked what they saw.

While some envious contemporaries expected the camp to cause Walter to wither, decay and pass into bucolic oblivion, their predictions were wrong. He actually was rejuvenated by the pleasures of Bell Camp and directed his business enterprises with fresh vigor.

During the '20's he was invited to make important trade speeches in Atlanta and before other bottling groups. He became well-known as a man of vision and a successful innovator in both producing and marketing his soft drinks. A modern fleet of four hard-tired White trucks had replaced Walter's "hayburners," and it was seldom overtaxed in distributing Walter's soft drinks. His market consisted of only 150,000 people, with a per capita consumption of just 32 bottles a year.

An astute, businessman, Walter used dramatic measures whenever the need for more business demanded it. All during the war, even when he had insufficient syrup to meet demand, he maintained his advertising program 365 days of the year. Once when local competition lowered prices on soda water and although he had not recovered from wartime market losses, Walter drastically cut his per case price from 80 cents to 50 cents. He weathered the effects of the price war for several months, until other bottlers had either gone bankrupt or, in Walter's words, were "willing to listen to reason" concerning stabilization of prices. The end result for the Mobile Coca-Cola Bottling Company was a recovery of the soft drink market it had lost.

Walter devoted much of his energy (he often described "intelligent energy" as one of man's strongest forces) to the advancement of his young tile business. He traveled as far afield as Pittsburgh to close out a "big tile deal;" and because of personnel problems of the company in Mobile, he nearly missed seeing his mother for the last time before her unexpected death.

Catherine Jean Bellingrath, in written communication with her devoted son until nearly the end, died August 15, 1922 — two months short of her 88th birthday and one week after Walter's 53rd. The pall of death snuffed a love that had glowed warmly and reciprocally for more than half a century. It was the end of a beautiful earthly relationship, but Walter was consoled by the thought of its renewal in the hereafter. He had lived beyond the physical reach of her influence for most of his life. Yet the separation never dimmed his appreciation of her sacrifices, fortitude and godly life. Distance never interfered with the constant flow of her influence for his good. As he looked upon her lifeless face, he grieved for the end of her long, unselfish life but was cheered by the flight of her spirit "beyond this earthly sphere" for a reunion with her departed husband and three children.

Was it more than coincidence that caused Walter to think and pay tribute to his father only a short time before his mother would be laid beside him?

> Dear Mama, [he wrote without elaboration] you know I anticipated the fine letter you wrote me about Papa's memorial scholarship. I knew what I had done was going to fill your heart with joy because it filled mine. The more I think about it, the more pleased I am, and I know what is true of me in this particular is true of you. It would also be true of Papa if he was here to tell us about it. In my opinion, the only way this old world is going to get back in joint is through the doors of the Church. What the whole world needs is a quickened conscience. . . . The girlhood and womanhood in particular need ironing out and recovering. This is

the reason why I am so interested in Christian Education. I hope and pray that the Christian Educational move throughout the country . . . will bring about the Christian reforms we all know and admit are so urgently needed.

The single candle Walter lit in his father's name to combat postwar hedonism through Christian education continued to burn in the memory of Walter Bellingrath. It was a light he would multiply a hundredfold in the years yet before him.

Walter's interest in strengthening the moral fiber of roll-stockinged, high-stepping flappers of the day was exceeded only by his efforts to produce economic gains for the community and all who would share the benefactions. He was one of half dozen or so influential executives who jointly used their specialized capabilities to attract new industry and payrolls to the area. To help accomplish this objective, Walter Bellingrath and his confederates pulled the fangs, in their opinion, of a major opponent of community progress. Their adversary was a strongly entrenched newspaper, with a publisher they considered obtuse and tyrannical. The group, including Walter, provided sufficient financial backing to start and sustain a second newspaper. This publication, *The Mobile Press*, outmaneuvered and outslugged the older one, nullified its sting and eventually devoured it. Mr. Bellingrath was a director of the conquering paper until his death.

22

WALTER BELLINGRATH continued to prosper and to
share the largess of his three businesses with Miss Bessie. His
generosity enabled her to trumpet more loudly at the walls of
the predominantly male fishing camp. They had not tumbled,
but many weakening cracks began to appear. She spent more
time at Bell Camp, expanded her visions and increased her efforts to improve the camp's appearance and to keep tabs on its
master.

When entertaining his male visitors, her husband used
whatever was handy to neutralize the scent of whiskey on his
breath, but his mouth wash was weak compared to corn
whiskey.

"Bell, what's that I smell?"

"Only Listerine, Bep, just Listerine."

"Well, the Listerine I use doesn't smell like that."

Miss Bessie's nose may have been occasionally pointed in
Walter's direction, but her eyes saw through the forests and into areas where rabbits could hardly penetrate. She began to
plan future development of the ravine cut by the unpalatable
well water, of the mill pond lake, of the multi-acre Satsuma or-
chard where the Parkers' vegetable garden once grew, and of
the river front with its dying clumps of palmetto.

All the while, Miss Bessie or her agents regularly traveled to
old homes in other parts of South Alabama, Mississippi and
Louisiana in search of large azalea and camellia bushes for
transporting to Bell Camp. Many were huge and of a venerable
age even before being brought to the Fowl River site. Some
people criticized Miss Bessie, behind her back, for paying ex-
cessive amounts for the bushes, but her friends realized the
overpayment was a quiet act of charity whenever she thought

a family needed the money which she could easily provide.

Because he always enjoyed travel, Walter's enthusiasm for Bessie's project began to mount when she suggested visitations to notable gardens in South Carolina, Delaware, Pennsylvania and elsewhere. Each time they returned, the couple was imbued with new ideas and a determination to make their place entirely different from others they had seen. The care and planting of shrubs and landscaping at Bell Camp became so demanding and involved, the Bellingraths retained the services of a professional gardener, "Uncle Paul" Thublin, to assist with the undertaking. He had been the Bellingrath gardener in Mobile and was called upon to sire the Bell Camp gardens.

By this time, Walter had transferred more of the affection for his late mother and other Bellingrath family members to the relatives of Miss Bessie and her in-laws. They were given positions of responsibility in the Coca-Cola and tile companies, allowing Walter more freedom for travel in quest of his wife's dream. In 1927, the couple took an extended trip to Europe. They not only visited celebrated English and French gardens, but also added greatly to their collection of porcelain, English furniture, silver and bric-a-brac. Included in the last were innumerable exquisite doll's heads which Miss Bessie garnered with childlike glee.

After the Bellingraths' return from Europe, they were not content to have one bush planted here, another there. Bessie and Walter moved aggressively and intelligently forward with an overall plan for beautification of a private estate which someday might embrace a residential showcase for her prized possessions.

To help add substance to their dreams, the Bellingraths retained the services of an outstanding architect and landscape designer, well known in the Gulf Coast area for the dignity and uncluttered beauty of his designs. He refined Mrs. Bellingrath's rough ideas, added many of his own, and major sections of forestland were magically transformed within a few years into both formal and natural garden areas.

Bell Camp was becoming a paradise; but, trouble, in the form of the stock market crash of 1929, forced its entry into the life of Walter Bellingrath. The Great Depression only wounded his

Walter and Bessie in Germany during their 1927 trip to inspect European gardens: at the old town pump in Lennep . . .

. . . and with relatives at the home of Walter's grandfather in the same city

Coca-Cola and turpentine cup busineses. People continued to consume nickel drinks, and there was still a demand for naval stores. But it was a different story for the ornamental tile business. Local and national building plans were shelved almost overnight, and the National Tile Company awakened to face a large overhead, a heavy inventory and cancelled orders from throughout the eastern part of the United States.

The collapse of the nation's financial foundations left Walter Bellingrath angry and dejected. He gave his best effort to keep the tile company in production but inevitably was forced to surrender to adversity. He soon overcame ill fortune, however, by converting the tile company's large, one-story building, near the waterfront of the Arlington area of Mobile, into a warehouse. He used that building and another acquired downtown for storage of cotton awaiting consignment to domestic or foreign points.

The Mobile Warehousing Company was the fourth commercial venture financed by Walter, and it operated successfully until about the time state-owned docks and warehouses were established at the Port of Mobile.

23

FOR THE UNINFORMED, there was a mysterious traffic snarl April 7, 1932, on highways going south from Mobile. Motorists who had not seen daily papers or listened to radios were puzzled by the unusually heavy movement of cars.

It was no official holiday, but one deliberately created by Mr. and Mrs. Bellingrath. For that day they had invited the public to share the beauty of their Bell Camp gardens. The response was unexpectedly great. Sheriff's deputies had to be called to ride herd on Packards and Lincolns, Model A's and Chevies to keep the intersections clear.

In 1932, Mobile had begun to capitalize on one of its richest natural resources: the area's acid soil, an essential component for the abundant growth of azaleas and camellias. The community became increasingly conscious of the multi-colored flowers and their ornamental value. And the formation, a few years earlier, of the Azalea Trail organization also stimulated widespread planting of the shrubs to help develop the city's tourist industry. While the gardens on Fowl River were beyond the reach of the Trail, Mr. and Mrs. Bellingrath were ardent supporters of the project and its sponsors, the Mobile Junior Chamber of Commerce. Because of this general interest in floral beauty, the introduction of Bell Camp gardens to the public was well-timed.

Provocative reports of the gardens' beauty and size, as well as its esoteric seclusion behind imaginary walls, had fired the imagination and curiosity of many. They now had a chance to peer over the wall and grasped the opportunity to satisfy their inquisitiveness as guests of the Bellingraths. Few, if any, of the visitors were disappointed in what they saw. The master designer, George Rogers, had achieved the miraculous. Flowing and cascading fountains, fed largely by the unsuccessful artesian well once drilled for the camp, appeared to be everywhere. The water-eroded ravine was a rock garden interspersed with ferns and mossy plants. Landscape improvements incorporating the natural beauty of the woods were exquisite, and concentration of azaleas and other spring blooms blanketed the estate with incredible color.

As the crowd sauntered through the central part of the gardens, they trod well-worn flagstone walks that seemingly had been there forever. These, too, were recent transplants. While azaleas and camellias had been acquired from nearby areas, the flagstones originally came from Europe as ballast for empty sailing ships that once loaded cotton at Mobile. Entire flagstone sidewalks, once numerous in the city, had been bartered and uprooted from city homes by Mr. Bellingrath in exchange for cement paving.

After that eventful "open house" at Bell Camp, the sylvan retreat of the Bellingraths was never the same. Requests for permission to see the gardens continued. Not wishing to be parsimonious with the beauty they had wrought, Mr. Bellingrath wrote this advertisement for newspaper publication on February 5, 1933:

> Although planting and developments are still in progress, and while the azaleas are not yet at the height of their beauty, visitors will be permitted to enter Bellingrath Gardens [the name Bell Camp was herewith abandoned] beginning today.
>
> In order to defray expenses incident to the protection of the Gardens, the cost of maintaining the walkways and roads and direction of visitors through the gardens, a charge of 50 cents per person will be made during the 1933 season.
>
> For fear of damage to plants, peacock, swan, geese, etc., no pets are allowed in the gardens.
>
> Visitors are requested not to enter any of the cottages.
>
> Cameras are permitted only upon written permission of the owner.
>
> VISITING HOURS 9 A.M. to 5 P.M.
> Tickets may be purchased at Entrance Gate

The entrance gate was hardly compatible with the luxury of the Gardens themselves. It was an incongruously designed, frame cubicle to protect the attendant against rain. A cigar

Frank Woodward, Mr. Bell's fishing guide and "man Friday," at the entrance to the Gardens during its early years

box served as the first cash register. Harry Sackoff, who had managed the defunct tile company, was the first manager, with Walter Bellingrath not-so-subtly calling the cues from off stage.

Mr. Bellingrath insisted that guest registers be used at his Gardens. While attendance was comparatively small, the old guest books attest to the broad geographical appeal of the gardens even during their infancy.

Once Mr. Bellingrath decided to go public with his gardens, he undertook the task of selling them with the same determination and energy he displayed in promoting the enjoyment of Coca-Cola. The word "See" replaced "drink" as the most active verb in his sales vocabulary, and he personally directed the creation of his advertising, some of which appeared as small space ads in a few national publications. Since the Gardens were not self-sustaining, Mr. Bellingrath financed the greater part of the cost of his advertising program either from his own pocket or with revenue from Coca-Cola. While he primarily was a businessman, Mr. Bellingrath never considered his Gardens as a potential source of income. They were a creation of love, not commerce, and his primary objective was to sell the public on sharing their beauty and the effects of his handiwork.

His love for the Gardens and his enthusiastic desire that they be universally admired sometimes clouded his business judgement and kept his local advertising agents, to quote one of his favorite similes, "Busier than a spider on a hot skillet." Whenever a severe freeze struck the Gulf Coast, an occurence not circulated or broadcast in those days, Mr. Bellingrath insisted on publishing advertisements announcing that Bellingrath azaleas and camellias had not been hurt by the extreme weather. Usually, these ads, placed in key newspapers throughout the southeast, had to be dictated to the papers via telephone.

There were no regular business hours for Walter Bellingrath. To quote one of his retainers, "When he hie'd you, he buyed you." He summoned associates for conferences whenever the spirit moved him; and some found, when Mr. Bellingrath was in residence at the Gardens, there was no darkness more Stygian or more eerie than when a pedestrian exit was made after the Gardens had been closed securely for the night.

The conduct of after-hours business once proved a painful and frustrating experience for Mr. Bell. One who often preferred to do his own thing, rather than leave it to subordinates, he left his office late in the afternoon and drove to the railroad station to pick up a pair of black swans. Their cage was strapped to the rear luggage rack of his Lincoln. Instead of driving directly to the Gardens, he detoured. A ground fog settled in, and betwixt the fog and the grog, he missed a turn near the Gardens and drove into a shallow ditch. His lip was cut when it struck the steering wheel. He walked to the Garden gate but couldn't give his usual signal for it to be opened for him.

"Damn it," Mr. Bell recalled, "a man can't whistle through his fingers with a split lip."

He couldn't whistle, but the black swans hissed angrily and often before they finally reached home on Mirror Lake, the converted mill pond.

The Bellingrath Home and South Terrace

Christmas at the Gardens features the festive color of poinsettias.

24

WALTER AND BESSIE now walked in beauty, but they hardly dwelt in marble halls. They had created the nucleus of a garden to rival many they had seen in Europe. But Bessie continued to remember the handsome manor houses and picturesque chateaux and enviously envisoned a comparable setting for her own treasures. The wooden Lodge and its refurbished outhouses now seemed offensively incongruous to both the Bellingraths. The magnificence of the Gardens called loudly for a home of opulence, one in harmony with its cultivated surroundings and forested backdrop.

The talents and professional skill of George Rogers again were retained by the Bellingraths, with the request that he surpass the other grand homes that had risen from his drafting board. In his plans for the house, Mr. Rogers subtly blended the cultures of several countries, yet he kept a strong flavor of the Gulf Coast area with his use of weathered handmade brick and iron lacework on the balconies and patios.

Plans were approved by the Bellingraths and work was started on the 15-room mansion in 1935. The building site, just north of the Lodge, formerly was occupied by two of the refurbished Parker shanties. Brick used in construction of the new home was salvaged earlier from a Mobile hotel built well before the War Between the States. It was demolished after nearly a century of lodging the great and not-so-great who visited the city during its golden years.

After approximately a year of construction, the Bellingraths moved into the house; the first meal was served in July, 1936. It was about six months later that Walter and Bessie left their Mobile home and moved to the Gardens. Orginal plans called for a south wing to be added to the building. This was never done. It is surmised that the original costs exceeded the estimates, or the occupants were satisfied with the house as it was. To this day, a second-story doorway leads to nowhere except a postscript balcony.

The years immediately preceding World War II were mellow, comfortable and luxurious ones for the aging Walter and Miss Bessie. There were servants galore — a chauffeur for each of them — as well as maids, a cook and butler. Mr. Bell had his loyalists among those who would help him hide his whiskey, and Miss Bessie's would ferret it out for her. And the mistress of the manor continued to make certain that alcohol was never served when the couple entertained. Mr. Bell's longtime butler, Luther Harris, was instructed always to set the table for 16 in the lavish dining room. That many relatives or other guests might not appear, but the table was ready for them. Miss Bessie's girth had increased substantially during her mature years, but size did not handicap her in running the household with almost military regimentation. The house was impeccably maintained. Her meals were a gourmet's delight, and service faultless. Her young nieces and nephews learned, thanks to the tutelage of Miss Bessie, a proficiency with two serving utensils long before some of their elders.

It was after the house was built, with spaces begging to be filled, that Mrs. Bellingrath began to acquire most of her antique furniture. She seldom any longer traveled afield in pursuit of her interest, but she was at home to almost anyone with something unusual to offer. The front porch overlooking the river was the "office" where she enjoyed talking shop with antique dealers and other tradespeople who called for an appointment with her.

Walter, meanwhile, enjoyed his Gardens, strolling about or lazing on one of the wrought-iron benches, anonymously chatting with visitors and basking in their acclaim for his Gardens. One such tribute, expressed by the late Sir Charles Laughton, he would never forget. The famous actor visited Mr. Bellingrath while he was in Mobile for a performance of "Don Juan in Hell." Mr. Bell asked him to sign the guest register, and Laughton wrote;

"How can I play the part of the devil tonight after being in Heaven all afternoon."

Walter Bellingrath's workaday world also continued to spin off both material benefits and honorary accolades. In 1940 he was named a director of the state's oldest and Mobile's largest bank, The First National; he expanded his Coca-Cola business in Mobile and on the Mississippi Coast; and was a dominant figure in Community Chest (United Fund) and YMCA work. His mark on the community was deeply and permanently etched, and he often was recognized as one of the community's most influential and respected citizens.

25

IT WAS THAT STAGE of World War II when audacious Nazi submarines slipped into the Gulf of Mexico to sink ships off the mouth of the Mississippi and near the entrance to Mobile Bay. The enemy, local war "experts" said, received reports of ship movements from a secret radio transmitter somewhere on the coast. What more dramatic place for it to be located by irrational rumor mongers than in the woods of Bellingrath Gardens, property owned by a man only one generation removed from the Fatherland. Earlier, a number of Germans and Japanese had been moved inland from Mobile for safekeeping, and some wanted the same fate — or worse — for loyal, harmless Mr. Bellingrath. One of the fictitious reports "authoritatively" had him turned in by one of his brothers-in-law, a native Englishman.

Mr. Bellingrath, who long ago had learned to deflect barbs of criticism, was more amused than angered by the reports. After all, he had been honored for his civic work during the first war with Germany.

Rising above slander was the least of Mr. Bell's worries. Gasoline rationing cut sharply into attendance at the Gardens. Sugar shortages brought on the rationing of Coca-Cola, and wartime demands for metal curtailed production of turpentine equipment at his Lerio plant. There were vexatious and worrisome days for an elderly man who preferred walking in his Gardens to tussling with governmental restrictions.

So many people were bereft by the death or injury of their men overseas that tragedy seemed commonplace during the early '40's. Walter and Bessie were childless and had no near relatives involved in the conflict. There were other than wartime forces, however, that abruptly and unexpectedly shattered the happiness of Walter Bellingrath and Miss Bessie.

About 1942, Bessie began to be affected by internal disorders that impaired her activities. Routine medical aid was administered, but specialists were consulted after several recurrences of the trouble. She was taken to a New Orleans clinic where an exploratory operation was performed. Upon her recovery from surgery, Miss Bessie returned to Mobile, to live out, her family thought, her allotted years. She presumably was not seriously ill, but Walter was extremely protective of her and curtailed the number of her visitors.

To give his wife a change of scenery and the benefit of a rest, Walter took Bessie to Hot Springs, Arkansas. She was accompanied also by one of her sisters. They were at the resort only a short time when Miss Bessie unexpectedly died on February 15, 1943, at the age of 64. The shock of her death was felt far and wide, and Walter sadly saw 37 years of a loving, understanding and devoted relationship abruptly transformed into nothing more than a melancholy memory. Walter had not attended church regularly since moving to the Gardens, but he had privately become closer to his God, who once again helped to sustain him in the dismal void left by Bessie's death.

Miss Bessie's funeral, as was expected, was attended by friends of hers and Walter's from throughout the Southeast. They crowded the parlors and garden of the seldom used Ann Street home. The tributes, both floral and spoken, were numerous and sincere, but none was more poignant than the ecumenical request of a Jesuit priest. He asked permission for several nuns from the Sisters of Charity, an order operating the Providence Hospital, to say the Rosary for Mrs. Bellingrath, a Methodist.

Permission was given without hesitation, but the family was puzzled by the request. The Nuns later revealed that each week Mrs. Bellingrath had sent, with only her chauffeur's knowledge and help, a clothes basket of flowers from the Gardens to flowerless rooms or wards at the hospital.

"If you seek a monument, look about you," reads the epitaph of Sir Christopher Wren in St. Paul's Cathedral. Walter and Bessie had often discussed with friends the possibility of their being buried in the Gardens. But Miss Bessie was adamantly opposed to the idea. She wanted to be

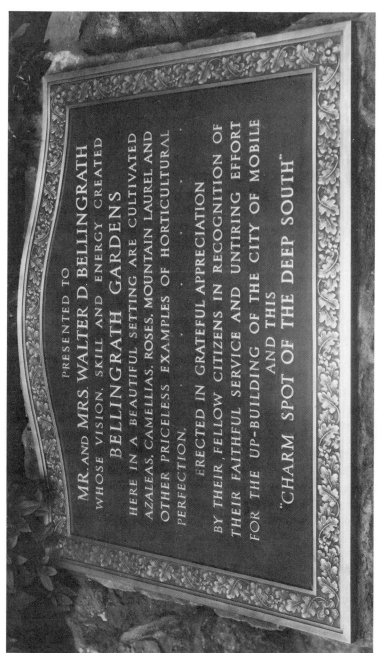

PRESENTED TO

MR. AND MRS. WALTER D. BELLINGRATH

WHOSE VISION, SKILL AND ENERGY CREATED

BELLINGRATH GARDENS

HERE IN A BEAUTIFUL SETTING ARE CULTIVATED
AZALEAS, CAMELLIAS, ROSES, MOUNTAIN LAUREL AND
OTHER PRICELESS EXAMPLES OF HORTICULTURAL
PERFECTION.

ERECTED IN GRATEFUL APPRECIATION
BY THEIR FELLOW CITIZENS IN RECOGNITION OF
THEIR FAITHFUL SERVICE AND UNTIRING EFFORT
FOR THE UP-BUILDING OF THE CITY OF MOBILE
AND THIS
"CHARM SPOT OF THE DEEP SOUTH"

A bronze plaque mounted at the Gardens by a group of Mobilians in tribute to Mr. and Mrs. Bellingrath

103

buried near other members of the Morse family. And so she was taken to her final rest in the same cemetery with her father (98 when he died), her mother and numerous brothers and sisters.

Walter, at the age of 74, was now alone amidst recollections that assailed him from almost every square foot of the gardens and home he and Bessie built.

*A portrait of Bessie Morse Bellingrath that hangs in the drawing
room of the Bellingrath Home*

26

MUCH WATER had gone over the dam of Mirror Lake. It was symbolic, also, that the thread of life supporting the ancient Parker Oak was being reinforced with concrete and cable. This last known reminder of the colonial heritage of the area was deteriorating rapidly.

Time also was a downhill racer for Walter Bellingrath, but the tenacity and strength of his spirit postponed the inevitable. After recovering from the impact of Bessie's death, he continued to direct the affairs of his regional conglomerate. It was not until later that he hired a full-time manager for the Gardens, and he continued to administer them from his "cussin' room" on the basement level of the home.

With the help of a series of well-born housekeeper/hostesses — the last was with him for about nine years — Mr. Bell entertained often and with finesse. A staff, sans Mrs. Bellingrath's personal servants, kept standards equally as high as those achieved by Miss Bessie.

Mr. Bell's love for his Gardens was so compelling in the late forties that he often quarreled, even in advertising print, with local residents for not visiting his Fowl River estate. He acted somewhat like ministers who waste valuable sermon time berating those not in attendance. And he once attended a Rotary Club luncheon and described the ingratitude of his fellow members for not visiting the Gardens, or sending their guests there, except during the Azalea season. His Gardens were like a beautiful woman, he often said, "with a different dress for each week of the year."

It was about this time, 1945, that Walter renounced alcohol for the final time. His mother's hand sometimes failed to shield him from temptation, but this time he may have reached for the hand of Bessie. He related to a confidant that Bessie once said how wonderful he was when he was not drinking. "Can you imagine my doing that to her!"

On another occasion he said, "It (whiskey) wanted to be boss, and I like to be in charge." Men closely associated with him during his final years said Walter never drank again.

During his declining years, Mr. Bellingrath's patience level declined. He became intolerant of business ineptitude, whether real or imagined, and his business affairs were in an unsettled state unusual for one who had reached so great an age. When asked the whereabouts of a former bank official he had hired to manage the Gardens, he replied: "One of us had to go; I'm still here."

James Street, the late novelist, tersely described Mr. Bellingrath during this period of his life. The brief profile of Mr. Bell appeared in a 1951 article on the City of Mobile in *Holiday* magazine.

> The gardens are sumptuous, breathtaking, but in many ways are not as interesting as Mr. Bell, himself a Mobile institution.
>
> For Mr. Bell . . . is a living example of the passing Southerner of the Reconstruction Era who, by hard work and hard trading, pulled himself out of the slough that trapped so many; his body as tough as a rail fence, brain as sharp as a brier, and his political and economical philosophy summed in the axiom of his generation: white man here, black man there — now fish or cut bait.
>
> He got into the Coca-Cola bottling business in 1903, which it came to pass, was somewhat like digging a shaft to a gold mine. . . .
>
> He is ready at the bat of his bright, miss-nothing eyes to argue business and politics as it affects business . . . and none of the New South's social-welfare trends. Economic individualism forever and white supremacy for longer than that. So fish or cut bait while the band plays Dixie.

Mr. Street's description of Mr. Bellingrath was not entirely inaccurate. But it was a superficial one. The brevity of his interview and magazine space limitations prevented the author from describing the spiritual aspect of Mr. Bell's life, his noble qualities of citizenship and his love for the beauty — the Garden for all Seasons — he and Bessie had created for the

*Tulips, more than 30,000 of them, take over the Rose Garden
during the winter months.*

*The famous Bellingrath riverfront grotto during azalea time
at the "Garden for All Seasons."*

pleasure of others from throughout the civilized world.

But, apropos of Mr. Street's reference to politics, a visitor to the Gardens commented to Mr. Bell that it must be heavenly to live among such beauty. "Yes," he replied, "it almost makes me forget we have a damn fool as president."

Mr. Bell continued to be outspoken during his old age, and he also became more generous. His private philanthropies, such as providing an elevator for an old ladies home, were continued, but they were augmented by sizeable public ones. The Chamber of Commerce wanted a large new conference room, and his church needed a new addition. His financial support of these and other projects made their realization possible. Both the Chamber and church additions were given his name.

A man who always looked beyond today, Mr. Bell realized he would not be on this "old ball" much longer. Childless, he reflected on the future and his earthly immortality. Who was there to continue the philanthropies that now gave him such unexpected pleasure? Who would keep his beloved Gardens, without adequate financial support, from reverting to jungle? How also to help perpetuate Christian values necessary for the betterment of man?

The quest for an intelligent, practical answer to these questions monopolized Walter Bellingrath's fading energy for many months. The solution would result in the most significant and far-reaching accomplishment of his life.

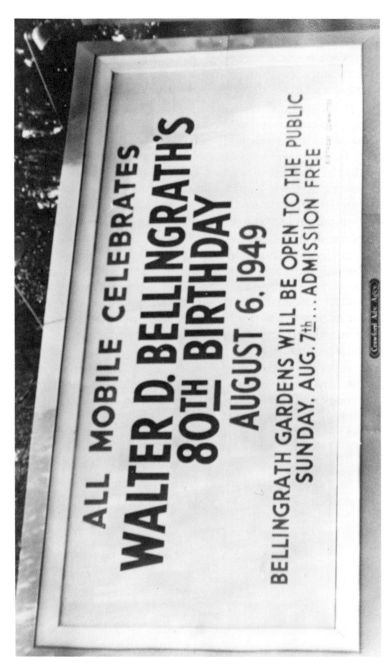

One of numerous poster boards inviting the public to Mr. Bell's 80th birthday celebration at the Gardens

27

DAWN BROKE hot and humid but cloudless and beautiful on Walter Bellingrath's 80th birthday. The date was Saturday, August 6, 1949, and Mr. Bell had planned a party. It was to be a capital affair and the most enjoyable of his many anniversaries. The public was invited to be his guest for the occasion. Newspaper and radio advertising was used generously to herald the great day. The idea of the open house was his, and he drafted the overall plans. Associates provided detailed support to make certain that he was appropriately honored, and that the event ran smoothly.

It was in 1932 that highways to Bellingrath's gardens first were congested by Mobilians eager to view the floral wonders of Bell Camp. Seventeen years later, many more vehicles — school buses, limousines, trucks, jalopies — jammed the roads leading to the Gardens. Police, sheriff's deputies or highway patrolmen manned major intersections to keep traffic flowing.

Much to his delight, Walter noticed a yellow school bus with Conecuh County High School painted prominently across its sides. It wasn't the Castleberry Male and Female School of his childhood, but someone in Walter's old hometown had not forgotten him. A contingent of students was driven the nearly 100 miles from Castleberry to offer tribute to that town's most famous son.

The fame of Mr. Bell on that date was spread well across the pages of *The Mobile Press*. Many columns were devoted to him, his Gardens and the Home. A six-column editorial hailed him as the "No. 1 Mobilian" and said he "stands at the top of the list in the field of public service . . . His foresight in industry and his business acumen have resulted in the creation of literally thousands of jobs over the years. He has shared his good fortune with many others, to the end that this is a better community in which to work and live."

A columnist of the day also acclaimed him with: "Mobile is proud of your accomplishments, Mr. Bellingrath. She is proud, too, of your outstanding record in civic affairs. And she is proud to be the site of the world-famous Bellingrath Gardens which has spread Mobile's name to the four and farthest corners of the earth."

Of particular pleasure to Mr. Bell was a letter one of his associates received from the columnist, Dorothy Dix, forerunner of Ann Landers and Dear Abby. Miss Dix, who had visited the Gardens on several occasions, wrote in her own handwriting: "I consider Mr. Bellingrath a prince among men and nothing would give me more pleasure than to lay my tribute at his feet on his birthday, but unfortunately for me I am in such poor health that I am not able to make the long, hot trip to even his beautiful garden, which is the greatest approach to heaven that any mortal man has ever devised."

"Heaven" on that day slightly resembled a fair or fiesta with improvised stands for free Coca-Cola erected alongside paths within the Gardens. It was a deliberate violation of one of Mr. Bell's cardinal business principles: never give his product away. If someone asked for complimentary Cokes, give money but not Coca-Cola.

Free refreshments attracted as much interest from the thousands of visitors as the summer foliage. A holiday mood was evident among those who attended the celebration. The crowd (about 18,000 visited the estate that day) responded politely, however, when brief speechmaking began. The old Lodge, at this time a gift shop, served as a backdrop for the podium.

Judge Ben Turner, Mr. Bell's lawyer and erstwhile fishing companion and life-long friend, began to give his farewell address concerning Mr. Bellingrath. His hands shook as he made his opening remarks. Unexpectedly, he lowered his script, looked over his glasses and said:

"Don't worry, folks. It's not nerves. I shake this way all the time."

The audience was his, and the ailing Judge Turner lauded the accomplishments of his old friend and entertained the

Mr. Bellingrath with the 15 silver loving cups received on his 80th birthday

crowd with humorous recollections of his experiences with a younger Mr. Bell. The Judge's sentimental remarks, as well as other complimentary words spoken during the day, brought a frequent sparkle or mistiness to Walter's eyes.

It was a day of fulfillment for Mr. Bellingrath. Sharing his pride was his Sister Kate, only three years younger and the last of Walter's immediate kin. She stayed protectively at his side or noticeably nearby throuthout the celebration. Birthday gifts included 15 matching loving cups with different inscriptions of tribute presented to him by the same number of organizations and friends.

There were other reasons, also, for Mr. Bell's contentment. The workable answer to the questions he had pondered for perpetuation of his influence had only to be documented. And he possibly had reached a private, difficult decision on future management of the Coca-Cola company.

Except for things left undone, it would have been a beautiful time for Mr. Bell to retire for the night and die peacefully in his sleep.

However, it wasn't the moment for a dramatic ending but for the beginning of a short sentimental journey. Mr. Bell revealed to a friend the contents of a letter received earlier from a town located in an almost forgotten niche of his memory. It spoke of hearing of him from mutual friends and of the reported elegance of his life and began:

> How strange it seems to be addressing you once again in a letter . . . I am glad to know of your success through the years and its culmination in the perpetuation of an earthly paradise for enjoyment of those, who for untold ages perhaps, will appreciate it as something of the divine *this* side of heaven.

At long last! A letter from his first love, Bethulia!

But she failed to say thanks for his box of Huyler's.

Mr. Bellingrath, after receiving his honorary L.H.D. degree in 1951 from Southwestern College at Memphis (Tennessee)

Postscript

Mr. Bellingrath died August 8, 1955, two days after his 86th birthday. His death occurred in the Mobile Infirmary, to which he had donated more than $25,000 for its construction. His last thoughts were for his beloved Gardens, as he died shortly after asking for attendance figures of that year's birthday Open House.

Following his delightful 80th birthday, he continued to direct his business affairs with forcefulness and an amazing sharpness of mind. With Judge Turner's legal assistance he created The Bellingrath-Morse Foundation. To it he left virtually all his wealth, including The Coca-Cola Bottling Company, Inc., of Mobile. Creation of the Foundation assured the operation of the Gardens in perpetuity and also enabled Mr. Bellingrath to continue where he left off in 1922: it was then that he first donated funds for a Christian education scholarship in his father's name.

Southwestern College at Memphis, Huntingdon College at Montgomery and Stillman College at Tuscaloosa, with a predominantly black student body, were named beneficiaries of the Foundation, along with the Central Presbyterian Church and St. Francis Street Methodist Church, both of Mobile. Mr. Bellingrath specified, for the schools to be eligible for the endowment, that each candidate for a bachelor's degree be required to take 12 hours of courses in the Holy Bible.

Mr. Bellingrath's other unfinished business was a complete and traumatic reorganization of his Coca-Cola company to make certain the business was in capable hands before it was transferred to the Foundation.

Since the reorganization involved the resignation of two of

his in-laws, it was an emotional and dramatic experience for one of Mr. Bell's age. But peace of mind and freedom to enjoy the sunshine of his Gardens, and the sunset of his life, finally came during his last few years. This was made possible by efficient, productive management of both the soft drink plant and the Gardens, enabling him to relax a grip on reins he had doggedly held for a half century.

Mr. Bellingrath was ill at his Gardens' home for nearly two months before he agreed to be hospitalized. He was removed by ambulance. As it moved through the gate at the Gardens, he weakly raised his head, looked out the window, smiled and gave a flickering wave.

It was a final farewell to his surrogate child — a beautiful woman, as he so often described her, with a different dress for each week of the year.

About the author . . .

HOWARD BARNEY observed at first hand "Mr. Bell's passionate involvement with Bellingrath Gardens. As the now-retired founder and president of a Mobile advertising firm bearing his name, Mr. Barney had the pleasure — and sometimes the pain — of creating advertisements to "Mr. Bell's" demanding taste. Mr. Barney's knowledge of Mobile's twentieth-century history is widely recognized. Aside from his years at the University of Missouri School of Journalism and a stint in the United States Navy during World War II, he has made Mobile his lifelong home. Before turning to advertising, Howard Barney was a highly regarded editorial writer and columnist for *The Mobile Press Register*.